Twin Flames Alchemy: Creating Heaven on Earth

Awakening New Earth through divine union

By Sujata Rath

Table of Contents

Preface

In the quiet moments of life, when the world settles into a soft hush and nature holds its breath, one can often feel an awakening stirring deep within—a call that beckons us to explore more than mere existence. This call emerges from the depths of our souls, an echo of our divine potential and the underlying truth that we are all interconnected. As we stand on the precipice of a monumental shift, a rising tide of consciousness flows through the hearts of those yearning for a new beginning, a harmonious Earth where love, empathy, and understanding reign supreme. It is with profound reverence and excitement that I invite you into the pages of this book, a transformative journey where we will delve into the profound mysteries of twin flames and the sacred voyage of love and transformation.

As we embark on this exploration together, it is imperative to recognize that we are not simply passive observers in this unfolding story. Each of us plays a vital role as co-creators within the fabric of reality, wielding the power of our intentions, thoughts, and actions to mold not only our own lives but also the world around us. In a society often ensnared by the relentless grasp of control, ego, and expectations, it can be daunting to break free from the constraints that bind us, enticing us to conform to a collective mindset that perpetuates division and suffering. Yet, the truth shines bright amidst the chaos: We are destined for greater things. We are twin flames, ignited by the divine spark of creation and designed to elevate humanity through the transformative power of love.

In this book, we will journey through the vibrant landscape of our shared existence, awakening to the beauty of our individual and collective souls. We will explore the sacred connection between twin flames—those destined partners who mirror our deepest selves, revealing unconditional love and spiritual growth. Their unique bond serves as a blueprint for healing the wounds of our past, guiding us toward a profound awakening that not only transforms us personally but also radiates outward to uplift those around us. Through the lens of personal experiences and deeper revelations, I aim to illuminate the path toward embracing our divine nature and understanding the essential role we play in creating a future steeped in harmony.

In this book, I have mentioned the unconditional love of authentic twin flames through a story. The ocean in the story represents the muddy world. The sea crocodile and the waves represent the negativity that disturbs the world's peace and creates chaos.

As we traverse the chapters of this book, we will delve into themes that resonate with the very fabric of our being. We will discuss the essence of unconditional love, how it can act as both balm and catalyst for change, and how we might learn to embody humility and empathy in a world that often encourages self-promotion and ego-driven pursuits. We will explore the impact of collective consciousness—how group dynamics and shared intentions hold the power to reshape our reality, how unity within diversity can build bridges, and how our thoughts and actions can create ripples of transformation that echo through time.

But it is not enough to simply understand these themes intellectually; we must embody them through our actions. Within these pages, you will find reflective exercises and prompts designed to help you illuminate your own path, encouraging you to engage in self-discovery and to share your experiences with others. Together, we will cultivate a sense of community that transcends borders and differences, fostering a shared purpose rooted in love and compassion. This is not merely a solitary journey; it is an invitation to awaken and connect with kindred souls on this sacred mission.

As we approach the culminating moments of this narrative, I invite you to envision a new era where peace and prosperity flourish—an age where love is the guiding principle, where our hearts beat in unison with the rhythm of the universe. It is my hope that through this book, you come to realize that this vision is not a distant dream but a tangible reality within your reach. Your journey toward awakening, understanding, and collective action has the power to steer the course of humanity toward a golden age of transformation.

So, dear reader, as you turn the pages, allow your heart to be open to the wonders of your own consciousness. Embrace the explosion of thought, the whirl of emotion, and the serene stillness that accompanies the unraveling of your own sacred journey. Together, let us rise, illuminating the world with the love of our twin flames and the compassionate power of our shared souls. With each chapter, may you find inspiration, hope, and the courage to join us in the creation of a new harmonious Earth, one that shines as brightly as the limitless potential resting within you. Welcome to the journey—let the awakening begin.

Awakening to Divine Love

Nature's Symphony

As the rain began to fall, gentle and rhythmic, like nature's heartbeat echoing through the stillness of the evening, the world outside transformed into a canvas of shimmering droplets. Sony stood at the window, watching as each blade of grass, each leaf, and each petal drank deeply from the generous offering of the sky. The richness of the Earth glistened, and the air filled with the earthy aroma that followed a downpour, carrying with it a sense of renewal and cleansing. This simple yet profound moment stirred something deep within, resonating with the quiet strength of the universe and the sacredness of all life. It was a time when chaos receded, and every sound—a patter against the roof, a rustle in the trees—invoked reverence for the delicate balance of creation.

Amid this introspective journey, she began to see the threads of divine love weaving through every element of nature. The towering trees standing sentinel with their roots entwined reflected the strength found in unity, possessing an innate wisdom that flourished through interdependence, mutual support, and an honoring of distinct roles within the ecosystem. Nature became a mirror, reflecting back what humanity often forgot: the essence of cooperation, the beauty of diversity, and the necessity of compassion in fostering an environment where each being could thrive. Yet there was more — the delicate balance was not merely a lesson but an invitation to awaken to the potential residing within each heart.

A Story of Unconditional Love

The rain continued to fall, and with each drop, she felt a call to listen more deeply to nature's bountiful teachings. So she walked out towards the seashore to observe more beauty of nature and its symphony.

Rain continued, each drop a tiny hammer striking the jagged coast of the Island. Sony pulled her worn jacket tighter. The sea, swollen and turbulent, mirrored the chaos inside her. She sought solace here, a reprieve from the whispers of a past that clung like the damp air. Her grief, a constant companion, had driven her to this desolate shore, a place where the roar of the sea drowned out everything else.

The sky wept, a ceaseless drizzle blurring the line where slate-grey ocean met an equally grey horizon. Sony stood at the edge, the wind whipping strands of dark hair across her face, tasting salt and rain. A sudden splash, a desperate flailing against the churning waves, ripped her gaze from the vast emptiness. A figure thrashed, someone fighting the relentless pull of the sea. A cold dread, sharp and immediate, pierced through her. Not just fear for a stranger, but something deeper, a pang of recognition that resonated in her bones, a memory she couldn't place. It felt like an ancient echo, a forgotten song humming in her blood. Her own recent sorrows, a tapestry of quiet heartbreaks, dissolved, insignificant against this raw, struggling existence. "Help!" A choked cry, barely audible over the wind's howl, tore through the air.

A faint cry, thin and reedy, sliced through the storm's symphony. It wasn't the wind. Sony's head snapped up. Her eyes, usually clouded with sorrow, sharpened, scanning the churning brown water. A dark shape bobbed erratically, a flailing limb reaching skyward before being swallowed by a wave. "Help!" The sound was weaker now, a desperate gasp.

Akash, he fought the current, a futile dance against the river's cold embrace. His each breath swallowed murky water. Panic, a cold hand, squeezed his throat.

Sony didn't hesitate. The chill of the rain against her skin, the ache in her bones, and the weight of her own sorrow— all vanished. Her feet moved before her mind processed the command. The chill of the water seized her, a brutal shock. The current fought her, a liquid fist pushing her back, but an invisible tether pulled her forward. Every muscle screamed every breath a struggle against the suffocating cold. The drowning person, a man, slipped beneath the surface, then reappeared, eyes wide with terror, dark hair plastered to his forehead. "Hold on!" she yelled, her voice raw, battling the wind's roar.

"Hold on!" Her voice, raw and powerful, cut through the wind. She shed her jacket, her movements quick, practiced. The riverbank, slick with mud, offered no easy path. She slid, scrambled, digging her bare toes into the earth.

The water, frigid and unforgiving, closed around her. The current, a monstrous hand, tugged at her legs. She kicked, a furious rhythm, her gaze fixed on Akash, now a mere speck in the violent expanse. A flash of scales, a predatory gleam in the churning water. A crocodile.

"Swim! Towards me!" Her words were choked, swallowed by a sudden wave. Fear, cold and sharp, pricked her skin. Not for herself, but for him.

Akash saw the dark shape, felt the water ripple with its approach. Despair threatened to drag him under. But then, Sony, a beacon in the storm, her face etched with fierce determination. He found a surge of strength, battling the current, ignoring the burning in his chest.

The saltwater crocodile lunged, its massive jaws snapping shut on air where Akash had been moments before. Sony screamed, a primal sound of defiance, and thrashed the water, creating a disturbance. The reptile, momentarily confused, veered away.

She reached him, her fingers closing around his arm, slick and cold. He was heavy, waterlogged. His eyes, wide with terror, met hers.

Don't give up," she rasped, pulling him closer. "We're almost

there."

The seashore seemed miles away. Each stroke was an agony, her muscles screaming, her lungs burning. The sea, a relentless adversary, fought them both. But Sony held on, a lifeline in the heart of the storm. They coughed, sputtered, bodies scraped and bruised, as they finally dragged themselves onto the sandy Seashore, collapsing in a heap. The rain still fell, washing over their trembling forms. Finally, they saved themselves. The journey was really hard. They saw at each other first time with little relaxation.

Their fingers brushed, a spark, not of electricity, but of profound recognition, firing through her. Instant soul recognition happened. It was him. It had always been him. The thought bloomed, fully formed, in her mind, though she'd never seen him before this moment. Inexplicable warmth spread through her chest, countering the ocean's icy grip. She grabbed his arm, pulling with a strength she didn't know she possessed. She felt like a divine energy helped her throughout the process. The ocean, however, seemed to have other plans. A powerful wave slammed into them, dragging them both under. Sand scraped her knees; salt water burned her eyes and throat. Her lungs screamed for air. *This is it, then?* a detached part of her wondered, even as her grip on him tightened.

Is this how it ends? Then, a surge of adrenaline, pure and incandescent. She kicked, fought, dragged him towards the shore, the effort monumental, each inch a victory. Finally, they lay gasping on the wet sand, the rain still falling, the waves still crashing. His eyes, a startling shade of green, met hers. A silent conversation passed between them, a torrent of unspoken understanding. "Why... why did you...?" he coughed, saltwater still in his lungs, his voice raspy. "I don't know," she whispered, the truth in her voice undeniable. "I just... I had to." A profound peace settled over her, an unfamiliar calm after the storm. It was as if a thousand scattered pieces of her soul had suddenly clicked into place. The universe, in its infinite wisdom, had orchestrated this moment. The synchronicities began to unfold like a cosmic scroll. Dreams, flashes of ancient landscapes, faces she recognized from a time before this one. Her body hummed with a new energy, a vibrant awakening like her chakras, once dormant, now pulsed with life. Telepathic whispers, faint at first, then clearer, threaded through her mind, not her thoughts, but *his*. His pain became her pain, his joy, her joy. *We are one,* the silent voice echoed in her mind, clear as a bell. "I feel like I've known you forever," she confessed, her voice barely a breath. He nodded, his gaze unwavering, a mirror reflecting her own profound knowing. "Me too. Longer than forever." The revelation of their twin flame connection wasn't a discovery; it was a remembrance. All the questions, all the suffering, all the inexplicable pull, now coalesced into a single, luminous truth. This wasn't just about saving a life; it was about saving her own soul, guiding it towards its destined path, a divine merging she now understood was the ultimate salvation. She looked at the man beside her, still weak but alive, and a fierce, unshakeable courage bloomed in her heart. She was ready for anything to do to bring him to a settled stage without anything in return.

The chill of the river still clung to Sony's skin, a phantom embrace despite the warm sun now drying her clothes. She had pulled Akash from the churning current, his lifeless weight a stark contrast to the life now coursing through her veins. A profound shift had occurred. Colors vibrated with new intensity. Sounds sang with hidden melodies. A strong bond is made between them, and divine love is awakened inside them. But this is the beginning, only the roller coaster ride journey has not ended. They went back to their own lives after spending some time of healing together as good friends.

But with this awakening came a shadow. They had to went through a huge separation phase and a hidden fight with the darkness as where there is light, darkness tries to deem. Both faced a series of negativities in both families with an invisible force. Her sister, always prone to melodrama, now festered in a perpetual state of victimhood. "You always get the attention, don't you?" her sister's voice dripped with bitter envy, a venomous hiss that made Sony flinch. "Always the hero. What about my struggles? No one cares about me." Her mother, wounded by her own circumstances, now wrung her hands, a constant stream of anxieties spilling from her lips. "The bills, Sony. The rising costs. We'll never make it. We'll be out on the streets. With this, how can you help strangers and not listening to us?" Each word a barbed wire, constricting Sony's newfound lightness. Even her father, stoic and dependable, grumbled incessantly about trivial matters, his face a mask of irritation. "This coffee's cold. Why can't anyone do anything right in this house?" Sony felt the darkness seeping in, a cold, cloying mist attempting to smother her inner light. It was a tangible force, feeding on the negativity swirling around her. She recognized it for what it was: an attack. But she would not yield. "I cannot carry your burdens for you," Sony stated, her voice firm, unwavering as she faced her sister. Her eyes, now luminous, held a deep compassion but also an unyielding boundary.

"Your happiness is your own responsibility. I am here to love you, not to fix you." Her sister's jaw dropped, a flicker of surprise breaking through her usual self-pity. "How can you say that? You're family!" "Precisely. And family supports growth, not stagnation. I am choosing to grow as I am born for a bigger purpose and can not be confined with those who never want to grow." Sony turned to her mother, taking her trembling hands. "We are capable, Mama. We will find solutions. Fear only paralyses us. Let's focus on what we can control, on abundance, not lack." Her mother blinked, her eyes clearing slightly, a tiny spark of hope igniting within them. "But... it feels so overwhelming." "It always does, until we break it down. One step at a time," Sony reassured her, a gentle squeeze of her hands. The shift was slow, arduous. Arguments erupted, tears flowed, but Sony held her ground. She set boundaries like invisible walls, protecting her energy while radiating love. She encouraged them to shift their perspectives by sharing her perspective and moral thoughts.

As the negativity receded from her home, a new clarity emerged for Sony. The drowning man, Akash, haunted her thoughts. Not as a burden, but as a resonant chord. She saw his struggles, felt his pain, a mirror to the darkness her family had wrestled with. He was still lost, still caught in the currents of negativity. She found him months later, adrift in a haze of self-pity and resentment, his eyes dull. He sat on a park bench, staring blankly at the pigeons. "Akash?" Sony's voice was soft, a warm breeze on a cold day. He looked up, a flicker of recognition, then confusion. "You... the woman from the river." His voice was raspy, unused. "Yes. I am Sony." She sat beside him, not too close, allowing him space. "You've been on my mind". Akash said, "Same here". But I'm nothing. Still struggling." He averted his gaze, shame burning his cheeks. "You are not nothing. You are a soul, just like me, currently experiencing struggle." Sony's eyes pierced through his facade, seeing the raw, wounded essence beneath. "I understand what you're going through. The world feels heavy, doesn't it? Like a constant fight." He nodded slowly, a single tear tracing a path down his grimy cheek. "Every day." "It doesn't have to be. You have a choice, Akash. To stay in the darkness, or to find your light." Her voice was a balm, a promise. "I can help you see it, if you're willing." His gaze met hers, hesitant, yet drawn. "How?" "By setting boundaries with the negativity that surrounds you. By healing the wounds within. By raising your thoughts, one conscious choice at a time." Sony's conviction was absolute. "We are meant for more than this suffering." He listened, truly listened, for the first time in what felt like forever. During the discussion, both felt as though their past traumas were merely identical, their wounds resurfacing. As she helped Akash to heal from childhood traumas by being a supportive listener without judgment, she gradually realized that this person was her divine counterpart. As she grew in wisdom and transformation, her divine counterpart underwent a profound transformation as well. Ultimately, she discovered that the person she was helping was an angel in disguise and that God was testing her purity through this process. She spoke of twin flames, of divine counterparts, a concept that resonated deep within his forgotten core. Their bond, forged in the river's depths, now revealed itself as a divine connection, a shared purpose. Slowly, painstakingly, Akash began his own journey. Sony helped him unconditionally in all possible ways as his mentor and a true well-wisher, not by doing it for him, but by holding space, by reflecting his inherent strength, by reminding him of his worth. He learned to identify the whispers of doubt, the hooks of resentment, and to release them. His eyes regained their sparkle, his posture straightened, a quiet confidence replacing his former despair. Akash liked Sony's authenticity and purity as he never came across such pure heart person in his life who could understand him well. Akash helped and encouraged Sony to achieve her dreams as well. Their union was not a whirlwind romance, but a gradual unfolding, a recognition of two souls destined to rise together. They became beacons, their combined light radiating outwards. They shared their stories, their struggles, their triumphs. They taught others to set boundaries, to heal, to elevate their consciousness. The Earth, groaning under the weight of collective negativity, responded. Small shifts, then larger ones. Communities began to thrive, and individuals found their purpose. The harmonious Earth, the heaven on Earth, began to manifest, one awakened soul, one divine union, at a time.

The Twin Flame Phenomenon

It is said that when the creator wanted to experience love, he divided his energy in two forms: masculine and feminine energy forms. So, twin flames refer to two halves of the same soul, separated at the dawn of creation, each existing in distinct physical forms but eternally linked by an invisible thread of sacred love and energy from the same frequency. This connection transcends dimensions, time, and the material world. Here Soul is considered as energy. For example, if you break a magnet, it still has two poles. A similar concept can be compared to Twin Flames.

Twin flames possess a pure state of energy with a higher frequency. They incarnate in the same lifetime and are destined to meet whenever there is a big shift required in Earth's consciousness.

In a world that often celebrates surface connections and fleeting encounters, the concept of twin flames emerges as a profound reminder of the deep, primal bond that links two souls destined to encounter each other across time and space.

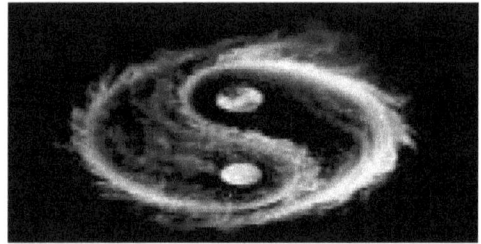

Twin flames are not merely romantic partners, nor is their impact restricted to individual experiences. Instead, they represent a grander cosmic design; a divine arrangement intended to catalyze transformation not only within the souls involved but radiating outwards to touch the fabric of collective human consciousness. In a society that often endorses separation and individuation, the twin flame phenomenon calls for a reconnection with one's authentic essence and the encouragement of others to do the same. Each flame carries unique gifts and strengths, merging once they are reunited to create a force potent enough to foster healing and expansion.

The twin flame reunion is neither simple nor linear. It is often fraught with challenges, internal conflicts, and moments of profound realization that push individuals to confront their shadows, insecurities, and deepest fears. This tumultuous journey mirrors the complexities of life itself—the beauty of creation intertwined with chaos, inviting each soul to embrace growth through adversity. Twin Flames are aware that facing one's own darkness is a prerequisite to embracing the light of their divine counterpart. The emphasis on self-work underscores the importance of becoming whole and complete as individuals before merging with another. Although the heart longs for union, the mind must be ready to let go of fears and egoic attachments that have held sway for far too long.

Intrigued by the dimensions of this sacred bond, twin flame love transcends the material realm. Spiritual awakening often embarked automatically after the meeting of twin flames by any means as per cosmic design which proves a real twin flame relationship, and the uniquely transformative power of unconditional love that blooms when these souls reconnect. Twin flames are mirrors for each other, reflectors of light and dark, leading those who encounter them into deeper self-awareness. It becomes increasingly clear that the twin flame connection is both an individual pathway and a collective evolution; their union serves a higher purpose that extends beyond the personal and into the cosmic narrative.

Twin Flames are incarnated on Earth in the same lifetime when there is a need of big shift of consciousness required. So meeting each other in a lifetime happens on divine time as a divine orchestration to awaken both for this divine love. Divine Feminine awakens first through self-realization, and she makes her counterpart awaken through her unconditional love. Divine Masculine awakening is more painful and time taking as per the divine soul contract as they have a difficult soul purpose to serve. Twin flames contain angelic energy and work as a bridge between heaven and Earth after their awakening.

When, during numerous reflective nights beneath the shimmering stars, Sony contemplates the divine orchestration behind her twin flame encounters. It seems as though the very universe is conspiring to bring them, instilling in them an intent that is both timeless and eternal. The chaotic nature of the world, filled with discord and division, aligns with a greater purpose that translates into awakening. As if by divine design, hardships encountered along the journey serve as catalysts, propelling the individual toward self-discovery and growth, creating a wake of healing energy that resonates with the collective consciousness. Sony starts to feel the pulsating call to action as they envision themselves actively participating in this transformative journey, fueled by unconditional love, compassion, and understanding. Their heart beats in resonance with the unending desire for community and collective awakening, feeling that every encounter exists to facilitate growth not just for the individuals involved but for all of humanity.

Thus, as Sony delves into the intricacies of twin flames, they cultivate not only a deeper appreciation for their existence but also a sense of responsibility. They understand the weight of their journey, acknowledging that every step forward contributes to the larger tapestry of human experience and worldwide consciousness. The inner calling that began their exploration transforms into a clarion call to arms, urging those awakened to gather in pursuit of love and unity. It becomes increasingly clear that as they explore the nature of twin flames, connecting with their essence is more than a personal journey; it is an invitation to contribute to a grander vision intended to ignite change within others and the world at large.

An awakening of this magnitude, she contemplated, is never solitary but inevitably rooted in the collective experience of those who share similar pursuits. They envision soul family gatherings where like-minded individuals converge, each weaving their narrative into a shared story of awakening. Together, they will celebrate, uplift, and resonate, creating an energetic vortex that fosters love, unity, and purpose. Sony, becoming a vessel for divine transformation, begins to feel the joy swell within them as they embrace the role they are destined to play in co-creating a heaven-like like harmonious earth filled with unconditional love and understanding. The twin flame phenomenon thus becomes the spark igniting a fire of purpose, inspiring each soul to recognize their part in a symphony of love playing out across the universe. It is an exhilarating beginning, breathing life into the vision of a collective awakening, one that radiates with the luminosity of a thousand suns, illuminating pathways toward unity and peace.

Signs of Awakening

Separation is an inevitable part of the Twin Flames journey for the self-realization and transformation required for the harmonious Union. During the separation period, Sony felt more deeper awakening. She observed nature so closely. That day, the rain softly tapped against the windowpane, each drop a reminder of nature's ceaseless rhythm, while inside, Sony found herself contemplating the profound complexities of her existence. That evening marked not just another day spiraling into the embrace of night but a reverberating call echoing through her soul—a call that stirred an unquenchable thirst for understanding her true self, her purpose, and the bond she felt with a force greater than herself. The signs of awakening were not merely abstract notions; they were vivid, palpable experiences that danced around her like whispers carried upon the wind. Each experience seemed to summon her closer to the radiant essence of existence—a journey that she now knew was resonated deeply with the concept of twin flames.

As she wandered deeper into the labyrinth of her thoughts, she began to unravel the significance of this unique connection. Twin flames—a term that pulsed with energy and allure—evoked visions of a relationship that transcended the mundane confines of typical romance, unearthing an arena where unconditional love flourished amidst life's most profound tests. The universe had created this partnership with deliberate precision, orchestrating paths to cross in a synchronicity that felt preordained. But what truly constituted the signs of awakening? What markers illuminated the path leading to the discovery of a twin flame?

It began with the inexplicable familiarity that surged through her when she encountered Akash—an unsettling resonance that sparked a recognition far beyond the physical realm. Her intuition, that whispering voice of truth nestled within her heart, often drew her to him, igniting a flame of connection that burned brighter than logic could ever explain. She realized that this recognition came with lessons, intertwined with challenges to confront her fears and insecurities. Each encounter introduced a depth of understanding that was accompanied by intense emotional experiences, often leaving her breathless, both from joy and from the weight of unveiling layers of herself she had long kept hidden.

The signs manifested not just in her interactions with others but also in moments of solitude where she encountered flashes of insight. Spiritual awakening often appeared in dreamscapes, vivid visions that dripped with symbols, messages from her higher self guiding her towards the truth she sought. Night after night, the dreams would unfold like cinematic tales portraying the journey of two souls traversing the highs and lows of love— showing both the challenges of separation and the bliss of union. She found herself waking with a sense of urgency, clutching the remnants of these experiences, deciphering their meanings like a puzzle that had been laid before me, revealing the craftsmanship of the divine.

In addition to dreams, she felt an undeniable shift within her energy, as if her spirit was vibrating at a frequency that invited the world's energies to respond in kind. She discovered certain spiritual gifts. The heightened awareness began to reflect in her daily encounters; she noticed an increase in synchronicities—those extraordinary coincidences that seemed too precise to be mere happenstance. A casual conversation turned into an exploration of shared ideas, words resonating with depth that left her in awe. Coincidences began to stitch together the fabric of her existence—the universe speaking in riddles that begged for interpretation, urging her to recognize the connections orchestrated by sacred forces beyond her comprehension.

It was as if the veil separating her from the divine had lifted, revealing an intricate tapestry where sacred souls wove in and out of one another's lives, each thread interlocking in unconditional love, compassion, and healing. The air thickened with an electric charge, a prelude to transformation, as she learned to trust her instincts and embrace these signs without fear. She became acutely aware that the connection with her twin flame was not merely an isolated event; it was a reflection of a larger, collective consciousness awakening, a vital piece of a grand purpose that elevated humanity towards unity and love.

As the flames of awareness flickered within her, she encountered others who were also awakening to their twin flame journeys. We often shared our stories like sacred offerings, our experiences echoing the empowerment of love, heartbreak, and reconciliation. These exchanges served not only to reinforce the connections we shared but also to remind her of the importance of nurturing our spirit when it felt burdened. The realization struck her: we are all interwoven within a cosmic dance, our souls begging for healing, yearning for connection on a level rarely explored in our human existence.

Through these discoveries, she came face to face with her own shadows of fear and insecurities, those dark facets of her being that had long been sheltered in silence. Awakening meant more than unveiling the joy of love; it called her to confront her fears and insecurities—the desires of the ego that urged her to seek validation in acceptance and recognition. As she ventured deeper into this process of self-discovery, she began to see that the twin flame relationship subsequently became a mirror that reflected her own truths back at her. In moments of confrontation, she would recognize within her twin flame the raw essence of every part of who she was—sometimes the laughter, sometimes the tears.

At times, this reflection forced her to contemplate the conflicting energies of love and ego—qualities that warred amidst the sacred arena of her heart. She understood that the more she illuminated her own path, the more she ignited the flame within her twin flame, stirring a beacon of hope for others. The duality of this connection, where we were both teacher and student, would be the key to unlocking new potentials for both of us and the world. Each encounter and every moment of introspection revealed a greater understanding of what it meant to authentically love—shunning the restraints of societal expectations and affirming the divine nature nestled within our spirits.

Thus, she dove deeper into this sacred connection, uncovering a wellspring of knowledge and awareness about the very nature of love itself. With every experience, she learned that love in its truest form could never be conditional or expecting anything in return; it flourished by accepting one another without judgment or limitation, inviting the essence of each unique spirit into a sacred dance. This understanding became the foundation upon which she began to build, brick by brick—creating a space where divine love could flourish unfettered by worldly constraints.

Amidst this process, the signs of awakening morphed into a profound sense of responsibility. She knew that as she explored her connection with her twin flame, she was aided by a presence that transcended the physical—an energy that felt both protective and guiding. It occurred to her that recognizing the sacred journey of twin flames was not merely an exercise in personal growth but a call to action. Each moment of awakening was an invitation to step into her truth, to share the light she had come to know with others who were also wandering in the dark.

The universe had moved through her, catalyzing a collective awakening; it beckoned her to rise and co-create a harmonious existence where love and compassion reigned supreme. She understood that her journey was not a solitary one; it was a bridge connecting her to the lives of countless others, woven together by the same threads of love. She felt the stirrings of a movement forming—twin flames and kindred souls coming together to embrace unconditional love as a catalyst for universal healing. Each sign of our awakening served as a resonant reminder that the power to heal the world lay not solely in the hands of individuals but in the shared vision among us.

The rain, now pouring in earnest outside, mirrored her emotions—each drop a tear of joy, of longing, of hope as she grasped the urgency of her awakening. She glanced out into the world, catching glimpses of chaos that still plagued many—a world caught in the grip of division, where humanity was often lost in the noise of the matrix. The signs, however, stirred within her a sense of purpose and transformed that chaos into a canvas where she could help paint a new narrative filled with kindness, empathy, and love.

She closed her eyes, feeling the warmth of the transformation bubbling within me, a call to be an active participant in the co-creation of this new harmonious Earth. The signs were nudging her to share her insights, to connect with those ready to engage in the spiritual dance of life, and to extend the invitation that all are welcome to experience the profound love that awakens the soul. She was learning—each day, each moment—that the journey of twin flames was not merely about herself and her beloved but about ushering forth a new era where love could flourish unbound.

In this serene sanctuary, disconnected from the cacophony of human strife, her spirit soared to embrace the beauty of nature. The symphony unfolded in haunting melodies only the attentive could hear: the symphony of raindrops composing melodies that danced upon the leaves, the whispers of the wind urging the branches to sway, and the silent, profound connection of all elements harmonizing towards a singular purpose—the pursuit of life, peace, and unity. The duality between the tranquility of nature and the turmoil of humanity struck a chord within her heart, igniting reflections upon creation's intent. In witnessing the beauty surrounding her, she pondered the divine origin of all things, drawing parallels between the infinite wonder found in the natural world and the chaos that so often colored the interactions among people. It was a contrast that screamed loudly into the silence, amplifying the lessons of love and connection that were as vital as the very air they breathed.

The Divine Call

As the rain subsided and a rainbow emerged, signaling promise and hope, her heart was further ignited with a vision for what trust and connection could manifest. The vibrant colors blending seamlessly across the sky were not merely an ephemeral beauty; they spoke of unity woven through diversity. Each hue amplifying the next; a spectacular display that whispered of potential if only individuals could see their intrinsic value not as isolated beings but as part of a rich tapestry of existence. Nature had always offered this blossoming perspective, yet humanity often turned away, entrapped in self-imposed limitations. The harmony of nature resonated at such frequencies; it became a blueprint for a new harmonious Earth, one where every individual acknowledges their role—even the fragile flowers— in the grand design, and where compassion reigned paramount.

Through this lens of reverence, the lessons of suffering and unity began to crystallize as she sought to discern the causes of chaos observed in the world. Humanity's struggle, endlessly perpetuated by control, ego, and superficial aspirations, stood in stark contrast to the enduring harmony and cyclical peace found within nature's design. It became clear that the departure from the harmonious path was marked by a collective mindset that fostered division, creating a matrix where fear could sow seeds of conflict and misunderstanding, leading to an imbalance that mirrored the discord in human hearts. In seeking solace from the tumult of societal expectations, she realized that nature embodied the antidote—a potent reminder that the greater cosmic dance operated within principles of love and cooperation, waiting patiently for souls to awaken to their true nature.

Driven by these revelations, she felt an urgent divine call rising from the depths of their being. It was a pursuit of not only recognizing one's twin flame connection but also extending the profound power of this journey into the world. Discerning this sacred bond with the greater universe—of being one with people, places, and all elements, felt like awakening from a long slumber into purpose. They knew that to embody and share unconditional love, humility, and empathy required recognizing and celebrating differences while empowering collective strength, allowing for an even greater harmony that mirrored the patterns observed in nature. The rain, which had served as a catalyst for transformation, left a lingering aura of anticipation: the world could evolve from the fixation on division to a celebration of life, where each perceived conflict could transform into a lesson of self-discovery.

In this newfound awakening, she found comfort in knowing they were part of something much larger than themselves. They envisioned a movement beginning to take shape—like ripples emanating from a single droplet fallen upon a placid lake, radiating outwards to inspire consciousness, engage hearts, and unite communities. It became apparent that personal transformations reflected macrocosmic shifts, and they began to weave their observations into a coherent vision to share with others, blossoming into radiant connections that inspired more than just themselves. Their personal journey of reconnection with nature served to kindle the hope for the world, evoking the courage to break free from the constraints of conditioned fear, urging like-minded souls to awaken to their individually sacred roles.

Ultimately, this journey through nature's symphony redefined not only her perception of the world but also ignited a sacred mission stirred by the interconnectedness of all life. It was more than an awakening; it was an embrace of purpose so intensely felt that every raindrop embodied a resonating truth— that love is the fabric of existence, bonding all souls to one another. As the last traces of rain vanished into the cloud-tinged horizon, Sony stood transformed, inspired to transcend societal limits, calling forth collective awakening, urging followers to join in manifesting a new reality painted with love, empathy, and boundless harmony. So, there beneath the endless, spacious sky, the spirit of possibility awoke—a luminous beacon for those willing to listen, learn, and ultimately step forth into their roles as sacred guardians of a new harmonious Earth.

Divine Merging

Divine merging is a milestone of the twin flame journey where the twin flames act as a pure vessel or instrument of the divine by completely in surrender mode following their intuition and maintaining pure soul energy. It is also referred as the spiritual union of twin flames' higher selves.

As the rain fell softly against the windowpane, tracing delicate rivulets that mirrored the thoughts swirling in Sony's mind, she felt an undeniable connection to the divine like there was a huge explosion of light within her. Something burst within her, and from that time on, she kept feeling her chakras spinning, particularly the crown chakra and third eye chakra with a surge burst of insights and clarity. Each droplet seemed to be a whisper of the universe, calling her to observe the intricate beauty of creation just outside her door. With each sound of rain hitting the earth, she could sense the pulse of life that thrived beneath its surface—trees swaying gently in the wind, flowers lifting their heads towards the sky, and the resilient earth saturated with the promise of new beginnings. This moment transcended mere weather; it was a divine orchestration, a reminder of the interconnectedness of all things. The creator's hand, so powerful in its ability to evoke life and beauty, shone through in this tapestry of nature that was unfolding amidst the symphony of raindrops.

Outside, the world appeared paradoxical; beauty and chaos coexisted in a dance as old as time. Sony reflected on how this abundance of life was often overshadowed by the darkness that human conflict brought to our collective narrative. It bewildered her how, in the face of such magnificent creation, humanity could be ensnared in cycles of strife, hostility, and division. She watched the trees bend against the gusting winds, their leaves trembling, yet they remained deeply rooted within the soil—a testament to resilience, reminding her that even amidst adversity, nature continues to flourish. It was a vivid revelation; the divine creation surrounding her was not simply an escape from the world's chaos, but a reflection of what life could be—a harmonious existence, unburdened by the egos that often fracture our societies.

Sony moved away from the window, the rain now a gentle murmur that infused her heart with a profound sense of serenity. Her thoughts drifted to the essence of creation itself, realizing that to know the creator is to immerse oneself deeply in the acts of love and compassion that create harmony. Each leaf, each raindrop, each creature moving through the world became an invitation to witness the grandeur of existence. The creator, an entity of limitless love, seemed to watch over us with unfaltering patience, imparting lessons through the miracles of our natural surroundings. She felt overwhelmed at how little we acknowledged these gifts—how often we brushed aside the simplicity of a sunrise or the intricate design of a spider's web in our relentless pursuit of progress.

Yet, as Sony sat there, she became increasingly aware that acknowledging and celebrating this divine creation was not merely an act of gratitude; it was an act of rebellion against the confines of our collective mindset. The chaos that dominated human interactions stemmed from a deep-seated separation—from the notion that we were all isolated individuals rather than segments of a larger, beautiful whole. This realization filled her spirit with yearning. She understood that to recognize the divine essence within ourselves and others was to dismantle the barriers that perpetuated suffering. Through this journey, she would awaken to the further truth that every act of kindness, every moment of shared laughter, and every instance of compassion could serve as a ripple, shifting perceptions and transforming our world.

With renewed purpose, she took her notebook and began writing down her reflections, and started to record the divine rhythm coming to her mind in the form of tunes and songs expressing the deeper love that resides in her heart. The act of pouring her thoughts onto the pages felt like a prayer; each word crafted with intention, filled with the light of hope. She explored the yearning to connect more profoundly with others, bridging the gaps created by misunderstanding and fear. It reminded her that every individual, like a note in a grand symphony, contributed a unique melody to the eternal song of life. She contemplated her journey, tracing the steps that led her to embrace her twin flame connection— the divine counterpart whose spirit echoed with her own. It was when her soul resonated with theirs that she truly understood the dimensions of unconditional love. It was an awakening to the truth that, like the creator, we are not merely observers of the beauty around us, but active participants in its manifestation.

In that rainy evening stillness, enveloped by the symphony of creation, she envisioned the potential of a new harmonious Earth where love and compassion reigned supreme. What if we could see each other through the eyes of the creator? What if we embraced our differences not as barriers but as the intricate threads that weaved our shared humanity? As she pondered these thoughts, she felt a flicker of hope igniting within me—a small flame that could potentially illuminate countless paths if nurtured with intention and action. The grandeur of the creator appeared to be reflected in the simplest acts of beauty: a stranger's smile, the first bloom of spring, the tender embrace of a loved one. It was these moments that made the world magical and, in their essence, tied humanity to the divine.

As the rain continued to fall and darkness deepened outside, she reflected on the call to action that seemed to resonate within the very fabric of her being. The chaos and conflicts of this world were a call to remembrance, urging us to shift our focus from the turmoil to the light that existed in every corner of creation. The sacred invitation was to awaken ourselves, to remember our divine purpose of loving unconditionally, and through this love, to play a part in the grand symphony orchestrated by the creator. There was a yearning within her to gather those who felt the same call; kindred souls who sought not just to observe the beauty of nature but to embody it in our daily lives.

She imagined leading a gathering where souls would unite to ignite this collective remembrance, exploring our shared commitment to healing the Earth, to nurturing one another in love, and to stepping boldly into our roles as stewards of peace. Such a vision seemed audacious yet necessary in a world entrenched in conflict. By embracing the magnificence of what the creator had woven into existence, she believed we could indeed break free from the chains of the current matrix—built on ego, competition, and control—and instead manifest an existence grounded in empathy and understanding.

In that moment, as Sony sat at the precipice of discovery, she understood that the beauty of divine creation is not just found in nature's wonders but also within each of us—the divine presence that breathes life into our aspirations, dreams, and interconnected relationships. The creator resides in the love that flows through us when we reach out to heal wounds, share joy, and nurture dreams. As she soaked in the rain-soaked evening, she knew she would step onto this path, carrying within her heart the flame of love ignited by the realization of her divine connection to the creator and to all of humanity. The world outside might be shrouded in chaos, but within me, a storm of hope was brewing, promising transformation, unity, and healing.

The Human Condition

As the rain drizzled softly against the windowpane, Sony took a moment to breathe in the fresh, earthy scent wafting from the damp soil outside. The vibrant greens of nature seemed to glisten under the gentle embrace of the rain, each droplet acting as a reminder of the world's inherent beauty. Here, in this sanctuary of life, they felt an unbreakable bond with the elements, as though the very essence of creation flowed through them, igniting a profound sense of serenity. Yet, this peaceful experience was overshadowed by the weight of humanity's turmoil that rattled the core of their being. In that stillness, the juxtaposition of nature's tranquility with the chaos of the human condition became glaringly apparent.

Thoughts began to swirl like the patterns formed by raindrops splashing into puddles. She contemplated the depths of suffering and strife that humanity has endured throughout history. Despite the advancements and progress made over centuries, the human experience remains riddled with conflict, struggling against the shadows of greed, ego, and division. They thought of the countless wars fought over land, resources, and beliefs, the ongoing clashes that brought pain to the lives of so many. Watching the rain cascade down like tears from the sky, they felt a deep yearning for connection, an aching desire to heal the fractures that splintered humanity apart. The dynamic forces of love, anger, fear, and hope collided within them, giving rise to an avalanche of emotions that could no longer be contained.

Her heart ached for those who were caught in the throes of despair, for individuals who lost their families in tragic conflicts or who found themselves battling the demons of their own minds. They realized that far too often, moments of kindness and compassion were overshadowed by the chaos of daily existence, drowned out by the noise of divisive rhetoric and fear-mongering that permeated society. A longing grew within them to awaken not just their own consciousness, but that of others, a desire to ignite the spark of love that lay dormant within countless souls. They recognized that healing begins from within, yet it must expand outward, like ripples in a pond, touching one heart after another until a movement of unity and compassion envelops the world.

With each flash of lightning illuminating the sky, Sony was awakened to the divine presence that surrounded them. It was as though the creator was whispering through nature's chorus, gently imploring human hearts to remember their sacred connection, to understand that we are all woven from the same cosmic fabric. The sight of the rain-soaked earth inspired them to reflect on how far humans had strayed from their essence; the chase for material wealth and validation often eclipsed the deeper call to love and serve one another. The environment was a mirror to the turbulence within – both beautiful yet marred by the scars of neglect and exploitation. A knowing emerged, one that emphasized the power individuals held to shift paradigms, to embrace a new way of being grounded in empathy, compassion, and selflessness.

As Sony gazed again at the lush landscape, they were struck by the resilience of nature. It thrived despite the tumultuous weather patterns and the insecurities that came with the changing seasons. In the same breath, humans possessed the same power to rise from the ashes of their struggles, to cultivate their inner gardens, nurturing seeds of love that could flourish against the odds. This realization ignited a flame within them, a fierce resolve to become an agent of change in a world deeply entangled in suffering. They reflected upon the stories that echoed through time—of prophets and visionaries who stood against the tide of despair, choosing instead to shine a light into the darkness, urging humanity to awaken to its divine potential.

In this intimate communion with nature, she envisioned a new heavenly Earth, one unfettered by the chains of ego and expectation that had long enslaved the human spirit. They understood that the journey toward this vision required authenticity and vulnerability, a willingness to embrace oneself wholly, scars and all, before extending that acceptance to others. It was then that they felt a surge of hope that, like the persevering rain nourishing the ground, the power of love could wash away the bitterness and pain that plagued the human heart. The realization dawned that each act of kindness, however small, would contribute to a collective awakening, a reimagining of the human experience, while fostering a deeper connection to both self and others. The narrative of humanity was not merely a tale of conflict and sorrow, but one of redemption, transformation, and the undeniable beauty of shared existence.

As the storm began to fade, they could hear the soft whispers of the breeze, as if nature itself was affirming the path ahead. In that moment, she pledged to weave their story into the shared narrative of humanity, celebrating the light found amidst the darkness. They felt called to embrace the powerful energy of love as the ultimate force of change—one that could transform the human condition from a battleground of suffering into a harmonious symphony of interconnected souls, each playing their part in an ever-unfolding tapestry of compassion and hope. The realization settled deeply within them: the human struggle was not an end, but a profound invitation to rise together, awakening to a new consciousness, ready to shape a future that glimmered with the promise of unity, understanding, and above all, unconditional love.

The Journey Begins

As the rain gently drummed against the window, a melody of nature enveloped Suzy in a cocoon of serenity apart from the chaos of the world outside. The warm glow of their small, ambient lamp flickered invitingly, casting playful shadows across the walls, while the fresh scent of earth mingling with rainwater effortlessly soothed their restless mind. Yet, despite the comfort surrounding them, a whisper, barely audible above the rhythm of the raindrops, resonated deeply within their soul, a call to action surging through them like an electric current. It was an awakening, an undeniable recognition that what lay before them was not just an ordinary day, but the beginning of an extraordinary journey—one that promised not only personal transformation but the potential to illuminate the paths of others.

In that moment of pause, Sony reflected on their life thus far, a delicate tapestry woven with experiences of joy, heartache, and most poignantly, an incessant searching for meaning. This quest for purpose, they realized, had always been tethered to an elusive thread—one that connected them to a deeper reality, a divine design that beckoned them to rise beyond the mundane and reclaim their inherent power as a twin flame. It was here that the significance of twin flames began to unfurl in their consciousness. They recalled tales shared in whispered conversations during moments of vulnerability, stories of harmonious unions that transcend the physical and venture into the spiritual realms. Twin flames are said to represent two halves of a single soul, split and living in separate bodies, yet eternally intertwined through love that knows no boundaries. As they contemplated this profound connection, she felt an overwhelming sense of purpose ignite within them, as if the very essence of love and unity was urging them to heed its call and embrace their sacred role in the unfolding of a new era.

The term "twin flames" echoed in their heart, a powerful reminder that they were not alone in this journey, nor were they merely a solitary participant in the dance of life; instead, they were called to be a catalyst for change, to harness the transformative power of love to transcend limitations imposed by fear, ego, and societal conditioning. This inner knowing began to take form, illuminating the depths of their being with clarity and conviction. She understood that the path of twin flames transcended romantic notions; it encapsulated a shared mission to awaken others to their divine nature and offer a seismic shift in collective consciousness. They envisioned a world liberated from the shackles of division and strife, a harmonious Earth resonating with the frequency of love, where each individual embraced their true essence and lived from a space of empathy and compassion.

Amidst this contemplation, she was struck by the realization that this journey would not be devoid of challenges. The collective mindset, entrenched in fear and control, continuously sought to anchor individuals back to the confines of expectation and conformity, all while perpetuating cycles of suffering and disconnection. However, rather than succumb to this daunting reality, she discerned it aptly as a challenge to overcome; a call to not only rise above the tempest but to extend a hand to those struggling amidst the storm. This journey would require them to embrace vulnerability, to stand firm in their authenticity while guiding others toward their own awakening. It was a commitment to embody the very love and humility they sought to inspire, and in this commitment, she began to glean the sacred nature of their mission.

As these thoughts flowed through their mind like a river, fluid and magnificent, Sony felt an imminent surge of motivation to act, to step into their power and awaken the dormant flames within themselves and others. What if, in this very moment, they could inspire even one individual to recognize their connection to the divine? They could ignite shifts within families, communities, and ultimately, the world at large. The flames of that love sparked a brilliant light within them, illuminating their purpose as a mirror for others to seek their own brilliance and remember their divine heritage. Resisting the pull of complacency, she recommitted fervently to their journey. Every step would be a reclamation of their sacred spirit and an invitation for others to join in the cocreation of a new reality.

With renewed resolve coursing through their veins, Sony envisioned gathering kindred spirits, like the pieces of a jigsaw puzzle uniting to complete a magnificent image. They imagined the joy of collective awakening, the connection through shared visions and intentions that could resonate on frequencies far beyond what the ordinary ear could fathom. They yearned to establish a community of explorers, brave seekers willing to navigate the uncharted paths of their souls, seeking liberation and embracing their roles as divine messengers of love. This revelation stirred their heart; the call to action was not merely a one-dimensional journey of self but an invitation for the collective, an opportunity to rally souls who shared the same yearning for freedom and transformation. How beautiful it could be to cultivate a sanctuary of empathy, compassion, and acceptance, to provide a safe space for others to bloom into their true selves.

With each unfolding vision, she felt an urgency rise within—they could not afford to hesitate any longer. This path would demand not only strength and resilience but it would also require them to strip away layers of societal conditioning and embrace vulnerability. To cultivate a community rooted in love and understanding would necessitate authenticity—a willingness to share their truth even if it felt raw and unpolished. It would call for transparency in acknowledging their own shadows and the divine light that existed within the depths of those shadows. To truly inspire others, they understood, would require the embodiment of love that transcended language, a love that resonated through actions, empathy, and compassionate understanding.

As the puppeteer of their own awakening, she could feel the tremors of a grand metamorphosis stirring beneath the surface—both within them and in the collective consciousness. The struggles and triumphs they would face on this journey, they realized, were not theirs alone. Each challenge would serve as a stepping stone for those who walked alongside them, illuminating the path for seekers yearning to break free from the confines of the matrix of fear and ego. They recognized that the universe itself had conspired to bring them to this point, where each experience, trial, and moment of insight coalesced into this singular, defining moment of embrace—a call to take action fueled by love. And with this intuitive realization, she knew with unwavering certainty that the journey had indeed begun.

In their heart, a fire blossomed; the promise of twin flames igniting not just within their own being but rippling outward as others joined in this sacred dance of connection and love. As the heavens opened above, pouring forth the cleansing rain that nourished the earth, they surrendered to the beat of their heart and the pull of their soul—the essence of twin flames woven into the very fabric of existence, urging them to embrace their purpose, unfold their destiny, and ignite the spark of transformation on a grand scale. With one deep breath, she stepped forth, embracing not just their own journey but the collective awakening that beckoned them to action, ready to bask in the light of love that would shine upon the Earth and nurture a new dawn, a harmonious symphony resonating through the hearts of all.

Breaking the Matrix

Whenever we imagine heaven or God, we look upward, and we can go upward when we are lighter. To become lighter, we need to let go of all dense energy like ego, attachment, or expectation and control, which pulls us down. By converting it to humility, empathy, and unconditional love, we can shift this current age-dense matrix to a golden era, and we need to do it collectively. Real Twin flames are rare and among the 1% of the Earth's population whose frequency resonates with this golden era frequency naturally. With the twin flames alchemy, we can inspire more spiritually inclined collective souls to awaken and resonate with this frequency to shift the Earth's consciousness.

The Illusion of Control

In the dim light of a rainy evening, with the rhythmic patter of drops against the window creating a soothing symphony, Sony found solace in the embrace of nature's beauty while grappling with the chaos that seemed to engulf the world outside. The tranquil outside world stood in stark contrast to the inner turmoil that arose from witnessing relentless wars, strife, and societal divisions that perpetuated the suffering of countless souls. It was during this period of introspection that they began to peel back the layers of existence, confronting the nebulous constructs that dictated human behavior—the matrix of control. This realization sparked a profound journey into understanding the origins and implications of this illusion that had ensnared humanity in a web of fear, mistrust, and disconnection. She pondered deeply, tracing the lines of history that revealed a narrative intertwined with domination, power struggles, and the collective ego's insatiable appetite for control. It became evident that the societal beliefs that shaped the fabric of their reality were far from organic; they had been woven together by those who sought to maintain power over the vulnerable, crafting a narrative that dictated how individuals ought to think, feel, and behave.

As consciousness emerged, Sony recognized that this matrix of control served to uphold a system built on fear and compliance rather than love and authenticity. Within the confines of societal expectations, people were conditioned to believe in scarcity, competition, and separation—ideas that propelled them to chase material success at the expense of their emotional and spiritual well-being. With each revelation, she was struck by the irony that while people yearned for connection and love, they often clung tightly to the very beliefs that drove a wedge between them. The matrix thrived on the illusion created by a fractured identity, manipulating individuals into viewing themselves as isolated entities in a dog-eat-dog world. It whispered insidious suggestions into their ears, suggesting that they were not enough, that their worth was tied to achievements and validations rather than the purity of their essence. The thoughts that danced in their minds mirrored the programming of the matrix, echoing sentiments of inadequacy and helplessness.

Yet, amid this realization came an awakening—an urge to transcend these limitations and break free from the shackles of collective conditioning. Sony felt a calling, an internal compass guiding them toward the vibrant realm of love and empathy, inviting them to embark on a transformative journey away from the grip of control. It was here that they began to explore the essence of unconditional love, realizing that love existed as an antidote to the pervasive fears instilled by the matrix. The compassion born from empathy encapsulated the essence of their being, calling them forth to align their actions with the inherent goodness that resided within humanity. She recognized that to shift the collective consciousness toward a more harmonious existence, they needed to catalyze change starting from within, radiating love and light into a world that had long been marred by darkness.

In the depths of their exploration, Sony found solace in the wisdom shared by their mentor, a figure whose presence radiated peace and understanding. The mentor articulated the profound idea that the matrix was not merely an external construct but also found residence within each individual, manifesting as self-doubt and fear. The realization that she stood at the crossroads of choice—a pivotal moment in which they could either perpetuate the cycle of fear or become a vessel for love—ignited a flame of hope within them. They began to actively confront the narratives that had taken root in their psyche, questioning the source of their beliefs and inviting radical shifts in perception. The journey into the depths of self-awareness became a wild expedition; they examined each thought that arose, recognizing its origin and weighing it against the truth of their divine essence. As they delved deeper into this exploration, they unearthed the understanding that love was not merely a fleeting emotion but a powerful force that transcended the confines of individuality, breathing life into the notion of unity and belonging.

She began to recognize that every individual was, in essence, a unique expression of the same cosmic source, a divine thread woven into the intricate tapestry of existence. This understanding compelled them to reevaluate the narrative of separation that had been instilled by the matrix. Rather than viewing others as competitors or adversaries, they sought to embrace the expansiveness of shared existence, promoting a paradigm where differences could be celebrated as a strength rather than a source of division. She sought to foster connections with like-minded souls, those who, like them, yearned for a departure from the constraints imposed by fearful ideologies. They envisioned a community built on the foundation of love and empathy, a collective that would flourish and thrive together rather than be compelled to adhere to the stratifications imposed by the matrix.

The process of breaking free from the constraints of the matrix was not devoid of challenges. She faced their own fears and insecurities, grappling with the remnants of societal conditioning that wanted to pull them back into the fold of conformity. There were moments of uncertainty, where they questioned whether their aspirations of building a new narrative were simply naive fantasies. However, a flicker of determination fueled their quest as they began engaging in reflective practices, empowering themselves to cultivate thoughts of love, gratitude, and compassion. They turned their gaze inward, striving to heal the wounds inflicted by the matrix, allowing forgiveness to flow where resentment had once taken hold. Through this metamorphosis, they began to recognize the unbounded potential each individual carried, realizing that the power to shift the collective mindset toward unity lay inherently within oneself.

As Sony and Akash immersed themselves in community-building efforts, they felt the momentum building as they connected with kindred spirits who resonated with their vision of a harmonious Earth. Together, they engaged in nurturing practices that elevated their collective consciousness, amplifying the virtues of love and empathy. They hosted circles of sharing, where they explored their stories, vulnerabilities, and triumphs, creating sacred spaces of authenticity that transcended the notion of control. In these moments, the lines of division perpetuated by the matrix began to dissolve, replaced by the warmth of genuine connection and understanding. Individuals who once felt isolated and alone discovered solace in the realization that they were not solitary in their aspirations; they were part of a collective awakening, a movement toward liberating humanity from the grips of fear.

The transformation journey urged her to explore the impact of collective consciousness on the world. They recognized how the shared intentions of a few could spark ripples of change, igniting a collective movement toward healing and transformation. In discovering the power of intention, they began to channel their energy toward collective manifestations of love and harmony, envisioning a world where compassion reigned, and the illusion of control dissipated. This led to engaging in acts of service, reaching out to uplift those still entrapped within the matrix, providing them with spaces for healing and reflection. The more they extended love outward, the more significant shifts they witnessed both in their own lives and in the world around them.

In time, her exploration of the matrix shifted from one of personal disillusionment and despair to a profound recognition of the sacred journey toward love and unity that they were now undertaking—as part of a larger tapestry of human experience. They learned that embracing vulnerability would not only foster connections but also become a means to touch the hearts of others, illuminating the path of awakening amidst a world clouded by fear. The journey became a testament to their continued commitment to rising beyond the illusion of control, affirming that the dawning of a new era lay not in the hands of a few, but in the hearts of many—each soul connecting in the vast expanse of shared existence.

In the culmination of their journey, she stood at the threshold of transformation, empowered to manifest a reality infused with love and empathy.

They understood that the matrix did not hold the final say; rather, the collective spirit of humanity pulsed with potential, waiting to be awakened through the pursuit of authenticity and connection. Through their unwavering commitment to nurturing love, their journey emerged as a beacon of hope, urging others to embark on their journeys of self-discovery, creativity, and unity. As the world witnessed this blossoming of consciousness, she carried within them the promise of a new harmonious Earth, a vision of sacred souls awakening to the truth of their divine essence and the limitless power of love.

Ego and Expectations

As she navigated the ever-complicated landscape of their reality, the concept of ego and expectations began to crystallize in their mind with an almost painful clarity. Each interaction in their daily life seemed to pull back layers of existing beliefs, revealing the insidious ways in which the ego governed human behavior and perception. They observed how preconceived notions dictated relationships, dictating rules of engagement that felt more like barriers than bridges. The patterns of communication were often tainted with a fierce need for validation, as individuals struggled to connect genuinely, instead opting for façades crafted meticulously to reflect ideal versions of themselves. In the throes of the matrix, so many were trapped within the confines of their expectations, not just of others but also of themselves, prompting a relentless pursuit of perfection that weighed heavily on the soul. She found it striking how deeply embedded these constructs were within the very fabric of society, dictating the flow of interactions among friends, family, colleagues, and even strangers.

Each day was a vivid illustration of this pervasive net spun by the collective ego, wherein individuals measured their worth against an everchanging set of standards dictated by culture, media, and, more poignantly, personal experiences fraught with judgment. Sony sensed a prevailing fear nestled within this dynamic—fear of inadequacy, fear of rejection, fear of failure. It was a silent tyrant that whispered incessantly, urging conformity at the expense of authenticity. They began to see that beneath this fear lay a profound longing for connection, a primordial desire to be seen and understood in one's entirety. Yet, this desire was stifled by expectations—expectations of how one should act, what one should achieve, even how one ought to love. It was clear to her that this collective adherence to preconceived frameworks not only isolated individuals from one another but also waged a war on the heart's innate capacity for unconditional love and acceptance.

As she contemplated this vast network of control, they recognized a pivotal truth: the matrix fed on the energy produced by separation, strife, and discontent. Ego thrived on discord, hoarding attention under a guise of nobility, often masquerading as ambition or necessity when, in reality, it was a hindrance to the soulful connections that the hearts craved. The weight of these realizations bore down, compelling her to reflect on their own experiences—the moments where they too had succumbed to the allure of ego-driven behaviors. It wasn't long before they recalled instances where their own expectations had cast shadows on relationships, creating misunderstandings that easily spiraled into conflict. This introspection revealed an uncomfortable truth; often, they had placed almost impossible standards on themselves and those around them, resulting in frustration and alienation. In glimpsing the tangled threads of their experience, a dawning awareness arose—a desire to transcend this binding narrative and cultivate a new path anchored in love, empathy, and kindness.

Determined to uncover the roots of this egoic matrix, Sony began to delve into the nuances of their upbringing, recognizing that many of the societal pressures and expectations were ingrained from an early age, molding perspectives that emphasized achievement over essence. Schools, families, and communities reinforced a kind of competitive spirit that prioritized success while neglecting the significance of vulnerability and the healing power of genuine connection. Rather than emphasizing compassion, nurturing, and mutual support, many were taught to pursue accolades, accolades that often come at the cost of true fulfillment. In seeking external validation through status, wealth, or recognition, Sony observed that love became transactional, a ledger of give and take rather than an abundant exchange. This perception stripmined the sincerity that should define human interaction, replacing it with masked gestures of goodwill often tainted by hidden agendas.

With this understanding came the beautiful yet daunting realization that the dismantling of ego wouldn't simply occur through willful intent; it would require actively unlearning decades of conditioning and forging new pathways that ingrained the ideals of unconditional love as a way of life. She envisioned a radical shift, where each interaction could be a moment to practice this love holy as the threads of connection were woven anew. If people were to transcend the noise of expectation, they first needed to challenge and redefine what it meant to love and relate to one another with authenticity. This wasn't just a personal awakening but rather a call to action—to invite others to unashamedly embrace their imperfect selves, no longer haunted by the shadows of their past failures and perceived inadequacies.

She became aware that love flourished when individuals loosened their rigid grips on certainty, allowing their hearts to whisper surrender to the unknown. It was, after all, in those uncertain moments where the magic of humanity dwelt—an unfiltered sharing of souls unmasked by the heavy coat of pretense. Deeply inspired by this revelation, Sony began to scrutinize their own beliefs and expectations with renewed vigor. How often had they stifled vulnerability in themselves, rushing to present a polished exterior rather than exposing the glorious messiness of human existence that truly connected individuals? It dawned on them that true empowerment came not from a pedestal of superiority but from embracing imperfection and the intricate tapestry of experiences that shaped each person's journey.

In this introspective fervor, she also recognized the importance of empathy as a guiding principle—an inherent ability to recognize, honor, and embrace the struggles of others. The truth was that in casting aside their own needs for validation or approval, they could begin to foster an environment where others felt safe to shed their masks. Empathy transcends the confines of ego, allowing genuine connections to blossom—hearts attuned to the same frequency of acceptance and understanding. Rather than competing for validation, people could create an ecosystem of support, where each soul would feel cherished and valued for who they are, rather than what they achieved.

With these powerful insights shaping their convictions, Sony felt an urgency to engage with their community, to initiate conversations that both challenged conventional narratives and encouraged a deeper exploration of self-worth rooted in inner divinity rather than societal accolades. It wasn't enough to simply reflect on these ideas; they needed to cultivate shared experiences that would bring others along in this transformative journey towards love. Consequently, she began to organize gatherings—a blossoming circle assembled on the premise of authentic connection, where individuals could express their truths without the burden of judgment.

These meetings created a sacred space, and in time, many began to share their stories and struggles, laying down the heavy armor crafted by societal norms. The rawness of vulnerability echoed loud in the hearts present, igniting a collective spark that manifested in resounding hope and earnest compassion. It became clear in these moments that healing occurs in community; when individual hearts converge, there's the potential to heal wounds not just for oneself, but throughout the community as well.

Sony envisioned these gatherings as catalysts for a movement—one that would transcend personal transformation into a wave of collective awareness, which served to uplift humanity as a whole. They harbored the belief that communities, empowered with the principles of love, empathy, and humility, could collectively unravel the egoic matrix that shrouded their existence and ignite a new era rooted in sacred connection. Encounters no longer defined by expectations, relationships transcended the transactional to foster profound bonds honed over the fires of shared experience. In this space, she felt a sense of purpose emerge, articulating the stirring resolve to co-create a reality where love reigned supreme, and ego dissipated like fog under the warmth of the sun.

Yet, deep down, they understood that this was merely the beginning of an ongoing journey. The task was not to eradicate ego entirely, for it had its role—not as a ruler but as an occasional visitor. The journey was one of finding balance, creating harmony between the sacred and the mundane, the ego and the essence of love. Continuing to confront their relationship with their own ego, she realized they would need to remain vigilant against the insidious nature of old habits that could resurface unexpectedly. But with each validation stripped away, they were piecing together a profound narrative—one that illuminated the truth that love, empathy, and the collective spirit could indeed foster the emergence of a new harmonious Earth.

In the unfolding of this vision, she felt something profoundly

transformative take root; an assurance infused within their being that, indeed, it was possible to rise above the matrix of control, emerge from the shadows of ego, and step exuberantly into the light of sacred love and connection. Their role as a beacon of this new paradigm was calling them forward, urging a deeper commitment to nurture not just themselves but the world around them. Love was, after all, the antidote they had been searching for, not just within their heart, but as the very essence meant to envelop humanity into a grand, harmonious embrace.

Shifting Perspectives

As the rain fell softly against the windowpane, she delved deeper into the myriad patterns of thought that had woven the fabric of their existence. Each drop seemed to echo the truth of their revelations, a gentle reminder of the interconnectedness of all things. In that moment of contemplation, the murmurings of their heart offered insights that transcended mere life experience; instead, they unveiled a grand tapestry intricately designed by the unseen hand of unity and love. She became acutely aware of the matrix of control that enveloped society—a web woven from fear, judgment, and division. It struck them forcefully, as if awakening from a deep slumber where ignorance had reigned supreme, to realize how these pervasive beliefs shaped not only individual lives but also the collective consciousness.

The realization dawned that to manifest a harmonious Earth, the first step lay in dismantling these outdated paradigms that confined humanity. The oppressive energy of control was rooted in a mindset that perpetuated separation—an illusion that discouraged genuine connection and empathy. Instead of viewing themselves as distinct entities striving for survival, they recognized the potential for humanity to flourish as an expansive family. This newfound awareness ignited a profound desire within her to shift their perspective from one of division to unity. In this transformative journey, they understood that love would serve as the guiding beacon, illuminating a path towards enlightenment and awakening.

Central to this shift in perspective was the cultivation of empathy. Sony pondered how simple acts of kindness and understanding could ripple outward, touching lives in ways that seemed impossible under the current paradigm. They began to witness the beauty that unfolded when one chose to step into the shoes of others—when the heart opened wide to embrace the vibrant spectrum of human experience. This process, however, was not without its challenges. Sony acknowledged that deeply ingrained beliefs often clung stubbornly to the mind, serving as barriers to growth and transformation. The patterns of criticism, unworthiness, and judgment entrenched in the psyche were tough to release. But by recognizing these limitations, they gleaned the courage to reframe their thoughts.

Strategies for embracing this shift began to take shape, rooted in practices that nourished self-awareness and fostered inner compassion. Guided meditations became a sanctuary for her, a sacred space where they could confront their fears and release the stories of inadequacy that had long dictated their actions. In moments of stillness, they visualized love radiating from their heart, envisioning it as a luminescent energy that enveloped not just themselves but the world. Each breath became a reminder of the potential for transformation, a call to collective awakening that rippled through the fabric of existence while transcending the limitations of the ego.

She also found solace in conversations with kindred spirits—those who sought to uplift rather than confine. They engaged in dialogues that encouraged vulnerability, sharing burdens and experiences that often went unsaid. By venturing into the depths of authentic connection, they witnessed how sharing tales of joy and sorrow invited understanding and acceptance. Such exchanges not only cultivated empathy but also dismantled preconceived judgments and biases that had been hurdles in their journey. It became increasingly clear that when individuals chose to listen deeply, they opened gateways to healing and growth; conversations thrived not only on the exchange of ideas but on the resonance of heartbeats, finding common ground.

In this unfolding journey, Sony learned the art of introspection, a practice that involved asking profound questions that stirred the depths of their soul. They began to differentiate between their true essence and the roles prescribed by society—unsuitable masks donned throughout a lifetime that had stifled their spirit. Who were they without the constraints of societal expectations? What did true empathy feel like, outside the parameters put forth by a world riddled with fear? These inquiries served as a mirror, reflecting their inner landscape and revealing the treasures buried beneath layers of conditioning. By recognizing their innate divinity, they uncovered the beauty of their unique gifts while simultaneously affirming the gifts of others.

As Sony embraced this journey of self-discovery, the need for practical steps emerged. They formulated strategies to cultivate love as an active force in their day-to-day existence, allowing it to replace the emotions that had long served their fears, such as anger and resentment. Simple acts of kindness became crucial in this transition—complimenting strangers, lending a helping hand to those in need, or merely offering a smile to brighten someone's day held profound significance. Through each act of love, she noticed the unshackling of their spirit—a renewed energy that blossomed within, transforming their interactions with others. It radiated outward like ripples on a tranquil pond, creating spaces of acceptance and connection that challenged the prevailing mindset of competition.

This journey also necessitated a conscious effort to expand their understanding of the world. Sony actively sought knowledge about diverse cultures, ideologies, and experiences, recognizing that empowerment bloomed through learning. They reached beyond their comfort zone, participating in workshops and attending community gatherings, eager to connect with souls who pierced through the illusions of division. Immersing themselves in different perspectives, they discovered that each story woven into the collective served to deepen their insights and compassion. The narratives of struggle and resilience echoed within their own heart, intertwining them with the greater human experience—a reminder that suffering was universal, but so too was love and healing.

As Sony continued to embrace these diverse connections, they began to feel the pulse of the community growing stronger—a vibrancy radiating from shared intentions. Here was the power of collective consciousness, an energy that harmonized disparate voices into a symphony of love. In such a space, individuals could be revolutionaries of compassion, leaders of understanding, and catalysts for transformation. They sought to inspire others to awaken from the slumber of control, igniting a fire that urged people to transcend the illusions of the matrix. By nurturing love as a guiding principle, each individual could play their part in the intricate dance of creation that was unfolding on Earth.

However, this journey was marked by setbacks, fleeting moments of doubt that surfaced like shadows in sunlight. She grappled with the haunting remnants of the old paradigm—grievances unexamined, judgments unchallenged, fears unaddressed. But through the lens of self-compassion, they learned to embrace these shadows, recognizing them as part of the growth process. It became clear that each time they felt an urge to revert to fear-based reactions, they could instead choose to breathe, create space, and respond with unconditional love. It was in these moments of vulnerability that she uncovered immense strength, discovering the beauty of resilience that lay within the human spirit.

Ultimately, the transformative journey to shatter the constraints of the mindset of control was a profound calling—an invitation for every individual to challenge the stories they had been told, to release the ties that bound them to fear, and to awaken to their true essence. By fostering love, empathy, and understanding, they opened gateways not just for themselves but for the collective. Sony realized that in each step taken toward this new paradigm, they served as a beacon of hope, casting light on the path for others to follow. Together, they could co-create an everlasting legacy of peace and compassion— the promise of a harmonious Earth that echoed long after the last raindrop fell.

The Power of Love

Love as a Catalyst

In the dim light of the cozy, candle-lit space filled with soft melodic tunes, Sony sat in quiet contemplation, a gentle smile curving on their lips, observing the sacred dance of shadows upon the walls. It was here, in this intimate sanctuary of the soul, that the understanding of love began to unfold like the petals of a blooming flower, revealing its intricate layers and profound depths. As they immersed themselves in this moment, they recalled the teachings of their mentor, who often revered love not merely as an emotion but as a potent catalyst for transformation, a force that could ignite monumental shifts within individuals and ripple outward into society. The poignant wisdom echoed in their heart, compelling them to explore the myriad ways in which love manifests as a sacred and transformative energy.

With each breath, Sony felt a surge of possibility coursing through their veins, drawing them into a tapestry woven with vibrant threads of connection, empathy, and kindness. They reminisced about the initial flashes of love igniting their twin flame connection, recalling how it felt like electricity crackling in the air, invigorating their spirit while simultaneously unveiling the darkness within. Love, they realized, had the extraordinary power to illuminate the shadows lurking deep in our hearts, presenting a rare opportunity to confront and heal our inner wounds. This embrace of vulnerability was not without its challenges; it required personal courage to acknowledge their own flaws, to accept the multifaceted nature of the human experience, and to recognize the imperfections that made them whole. By allowing love to inspire their journey, they were ultimately gifted with profound self-discovery and growth, a blossoming that encouraged them to foster a deeper understanding of themselves and others.

As Sony sat in this contemplative reverie, it became increasingly clear that love's ability to heal extended far beyond the individual realm. They pondered the collective struggles witnessed in communities globally, marked by strife and division, really a reflection of humanity's struggle to embody unconditional love. The world, too often governed by fear, resentment, and ego, became a breeding ground for conflict. As they opened themselves to explore this collective narrative woven through historical events and present-day realities, Sony saw love as an essential balm, a remedy capable of smoothing the jagged edges of discord if only more souls were willing to embrace it boldly. Love's multifaceted nature mirrored the transformative light of the universe, radiating warmth and hope and capable of binding together the fragmented pieces of society through acts of compassion, understanding, and shared purpose.

Sony envisioned a world where kindness flowed as effortlessly as rivers winding through valleys, nourishing all it encountered along the way. They contemplated the beauty of connections formed through small acts: a smile exchanged with a stranger, a helping hand offered to someone in need, or the shared laughter of friends. Each act of love built invisible bridges between hearts, weaving a resilient fabric of unity that could withstand the harsh winds of separation and individuality. Love fortified the spirit, reminding people that they were not alone in their struggles, empowering them to rise above the challenges they faced together. They could see that love had the power to create ripples that transformed lives, communities, and eventually the world. In those moments of clarity, a vision unlike any they had experienced began to crystallize—of a harmonious Earth co-created through collective love and empathy.

With this realization, Sony felt prompted to examine deeper truths within themselves and around them. Love, they recognized, was not a static entity but a continuous force of creation and renewal, providing sustenance and security to the spirit while inviting individuals to become the architects of their own realities. This understanding invited them to consider how love is like a garden's ecosystem; it requires nurturing, attention, and the willingness to adapt to changing seasons. In cultivating support for others, they discovered, powered by love and a desire to help heal the world, they were contributing to something much grander than their own individual journey. The interconnectedness of all souls resonated in their heart, urging them to dig deeper into what love could foster in communal spaces, uniting people in a shared intent to uplift humanity.

Sony vividly recalled an experience from their past when they attended a gathering of like-minded individuals dedicated to spiritual growth and the power of love. Within that circle, there was palpable energy—a resonance not only of shared beliefs but also the desire to enact change within the broader world. Among those gathered souls, Sony felt at home, as if each person was an integral piece mysteriously coming together to form a magnificent mosaic.

Through prayers, affirmations, and collective intentions spoken in unison, they witnessed the tangible impact of love in this environment, as it transformed the energy from individual aspirations to a unified voice calling for peace and healing. In those moments of sacred connection, they felt as if every whispered wish and heartfelt prayer sent ripples of love into the universe, contributing to a collective awakening that transcended boundaries. It was in that collective experience that she recognized love could serve as the ignition source in a fire that would eventually blaze with the vigor of transformation and renewal.

Drawing from this vision of interconnected souls, Sony knew they could not hoard the essence of love for themselves; instead, they were called to embody it fully. Love was meant to be shared, to be radiated to all corners of their world, transcending barriers and illuminating the darkest places. But how could they inspire others to join this vital journey? They were eager to embark on their own quest of spreading love, to spark a movement that resonated with the authenticity of their heart's yearnings. They envisioned creating safe spaces where community members could share their stories, learn from one another, and nurture the collective spark of love. The thought of leading meditation gatherings, holding workshops focused on inner healing, or organizing outreach programs filled them with joy. Even simple acts like engaging with local charities or planting community gardens could engage the tangibility of love as a catalyst for healing the world.

As their mind brimmed with ideas of growth and community, Sony began to appreciate the beauty of vulnerability as they reached out to others. They acknowledged that love would invariably call them to confront their own fears and insecurities, to remove the veils they had hidden behind out of habit. But with every challenge come opportunities for growth, and despite the uneasiness, they recognized that true strength emerged in moments of vulnerability. The desire to inspire others to embrace the inherent interconnectedness of humanity fueled her courage. As they engaged in conversations, fostered projects rooted in love, and nurtured bonds of empathy, they learned that each interaction could sow—a small but significant seed in the flourishing soil of collective consciousness.

They tirelessly prepared for the projects that eagerly echoed in their heart, realizing that love can pull people out of their shells, inviting them to courageously share their own stories, which can bind the collective human experience inseparably. One day, on a sunny afternoon alongside friends and fellow seekers, they initiated a community gathering that aimed to embrace love as the force that unites. The air buzzed with excitement, and a warm glow enveloped the participants as they started sharing their personal journeys—each story woven with threads of pain and beauty. As emotions rose and fell like the gentle waves of the ocean, the feeling of collective healing coursed through the assembly, resonating deeply. Each word exchanged, and tear shed became part of a shared narrative of resilience and hope. In that moment, they could witness the transformative power of love as it shifted old paradigms away from isolation and fragmentation toward an embrace of unity, fostering growth together.

Through this sacred gathering, Sony observed how the hearts of the attendees began to reawaken as they ignited discussions of restorative justice, accountability, and compassion. Love indeed acted as the catalyst, manifesting through dialogues that crossed boundaries and perspectives. It became evident that healing was not a distant dream; it had sprouted amid the commitment to raise awareness and cultivate a shared consciousness. Each encounter served as a reminder of the vibrant life force emitted when hearts chose to connect, uplift, and inspire one another. In that circle of friends, family, mentors, and newfound souls, love emerged as the unsung hero of collective healing—an energy bound not by romantic entanglements but by a universal acknowledgment that humanity exists as a tapestry of experiences, every single thread contributing to the creation of something finer than the individual.

Just like that, love became an indulgence, a celebration of the essential bond shared among all beings—a call to collectively heal the wounds of a society that often forgets the beauty in connection. Carrying this profound love forward, Sony embraced their newfound role as a guide, empowering others to recognize their own divine nature and spark their flames, inviting their unique expressions of love into the world. Every heart, they realized, holds within realms of potential waiting to be released. It was in this phase of exploration, of communal steps taken together toward transformation that she felt a sense of awakening, as if the very world around them was waiting for those willing to bravely step into their essence and reveal the light that could guide others toward healing, unity, and profound change.

The journey of love, thus, became one of heart and spirit—a binding force through which each individual could play their part in co-creating a harmonious Earth. Sony marveled at the enormity of this realization, understanding that love demanded not mere voice but action, each showing up for one another in authentic ways to work toward peace and growth. Love, after all, was the quintessential catalyst that could shatter the confines of the current matrix built on fear, control, and expectations. As they engaged further in this sacred mission, she understood this unwavering nature of love could inspire waves of change — through community connections, through acts of kindness, and through the legacy of shared purpose. Each step taken in love, whether small or monumental, would always carry the capacity to create a transformation that resounds for generations to come, a testament to the eternal truth that love is indeed the most powerful force of all.

Healing through Love

The journey toward understanding the healing power of love begins with a deep internal exploration, where Sony finds themselves reflecting on the intricate patterns of human emotions. Love, often viewed merely as a feeling, uncovers itself as a profound force, a cosmic energy capable of mending broken hearts, bridging divides, and transforming lives. As the rain softly taps against the window, framing a serene backdrop, she envisions the ripple effects of genuine love cascading through the fabric of existence. They realize that every act of kindness, every moment of compassion, contributes to the healing tapestry of the universe. It dawns on them that love is not only a balm for individual wounds but a powerful catalyst for collective healing, a truth that resonates deeply within their spirit.

Delving further into this mystical understanding, she recalls conversations with their mentor, who spoke of love as a vibration—an energy frequency that elevates consciousness and opens pathways for healing. This vibration can dissolve the barriers erected by fear, resentment, and misunderstandings. Each person carries their own set of wounds—those inflicted by past traumas, societal judgments, and the painful expectations that often plague our hearts. Sony understands that to heal is to acknowledge these wounds, to bring them into the light of awareness rather than allowing them to fester in the corners of the mind. In this process, love serves as the guiding force, encouraging vulnerability and honesty. It is when we dare to enter the depths of our pain, surrounded by the embrace of love, that true healing can begin. Sony realizes that by sharing their own wounds, they invite others to do the same, creating a space that fosters understanding and acceptance.

Drawing lessons from nature, she observes how the seasons play a role in the cycle of healing. Just as spring follows winter, bringing forth renewal and vibrant blossoms, so too must humans allow their souls to go through cycles of introspection and regeneration. Each emotion experienced, whether joy, sadness, or anger, is a part of the crucial process toward reclaiming wholeness. Love nurtures this cycle; it teaches us to honor our emotions as indicators of our internal landscape, guiding us to confront the shadows lodged within. By embracing love, both for ourselves and others, we begin to transmute the energies that have long caused suffering into forces of empowerment and strength. It becomes evident that the work of healing is not a solitary path but a communal journey, woven together by the threads of shared experiences and vulnerabilities.

It is during a gathering of like-minded souls that she witnesses first-hand the collective power of love in healing. As participants share their stories—their struggles, their triumphs, they realize that each narrative carries a unique essence yet resonates on a fundamental level, echoing a universal human experience. Such gatherings ignite the spirit of unity, a reminder that healing occurs when we courageously reveal our truths and listen deeply to others. In the harmonizing presence of full hearts, the energy shifts; wounds transform into wisdom, and pain evolves into purpose. Sony recognizes that these meetings, filled with authenticity and empathy, lay the groundwork for a vast network of love—one where personal healing fuels collective transformation.

She reflects upon their own healing journey, understanding the challenges that arise when one attempts to confront their fears and insecurities. Fear often acts as a barrier, holding individuals hostage in a prison of emotional isolation. Yet, through the lens of love, fear begins to lose its grip. Sony recalls moments of personal transformation, instances where they stepped into the light of vulnerability, sharing their inner battles with trusted companions. These moments crystallized the understanding that love can often be the most potent antidote to fear. When surrounded by a nurturing community, the act of sharing becomes an embodiment of love itself; it dissolves the isolation that fear breeds and nourishes the collective spirit.

To further explore methods of healing through love, Sony engages in practices that deepen their connection to this transformative energy. They find solace in meditation, where intentional moments of quietude allow the heart to open and soften. In these still spaces, they visualized love as a radiant light enveloping their body, washing over their past wounds like a gentle wave. Breathing deeply, they become aware of how love invites forgiveness—not just towards others, but also towards oneself. Each inhalation brings in renewed energy, while each exhalation releases what no longer serves them, including old grudges and pain. This practice of compassionate self-forgiveness enables her to experience a profound liberation, connecting them to the essence of love that lies within.

Beyond the solitude of personal meditation, she also engages in service as a means of healing—an act that actualizes love into tangible forms. They volunteer at local shelters, offering support to those facing hardship, sharing meals, warm embraces, and words of encouragement. Through these interactions, she learns firsthand that love is magnified when it is given away. Each smile exchanged, each act of kindness rippling outward, creates a resonance that reverberates throughout the community. Sony feels enriched, finding that through service, they heal both others and themselves. They come to understand that love's ability to heal grows exponentially when its energy is channeled into the service of others, reinforcing not only their own sense of purpose but the interconnectedness of all humanity.

Recalling these experiences, Sony writes about the power of art as another medium for healing through love. Creating art becomes an act of love—a way to express feelings that might otherwise remain trapped in silence. Whether through painting, writing, or music, the act of creation becomes a sacred dialogue between the self and the universe. They encourage the reader to explore their own creativity as a healing balm, connecting deeply with their inner essence and allowing love to flow through their work. She asserts that art provides a vessel for healing by transforming suffering into beauty, inviting others to resonate with their emotions and stories. In envisioning this process of creation, she recognizes that artistic expressions can bridge divides, fostering empathy between diverse individuals who find solace in shared human experiences.

As Sony continues this exploration of love's healing methods, they come across ancient wisdom, understanding the role of rituals and ceremonies in bringing communities together for collective healing. They learn about the significance of creating sacred spaces where intentions can be set and energies aligned. Cultural rituals, whether through threads of spirituality or traditions, offer frameworks for individuals to connect with one another and engage in healing processes. By sharing love in these ceremonial moments, communities can harness their collective power, amplifying healing energies that transcend individual experiences. It dawns upon her that as they initiate their own rituals— simple meditative gatherings under the stars or potlucks of shared stories—they can foster a sense of belonging and unity that facilitates healing.

Ultimately, Sony comes to realize that the power of love in healing is not just an abstract concept; it is rooted in action, in daily choices that allow individuals to express their love more authentically. Whether by choosing to forgive, practicing gratitude, serving others, honoring creativity, or participating in community rituals, love can become a resounding anthem that echoes through the heart of humanity. She sees that while the journey of healing may seem daunting, it is illuminated by the gentle light of love, motoring us forward, guiding us through the shadows. Embracing the power of love allows us to reclaim not just our personal stories but to forge a new narrative for the world—one rooted in compassion, connection, and a shared vision for a harmonious Earth. This realization becomes a potent inspiration, propelling her to share their insights with others, urging them to recognize the profound healing gifts that lie within love, waiting to be unleashed for the upliftment of all. Through such revelations, she embraces the transformative potential that resides in every heart, affirming that love is indeed the most potent medicine available to heal our wounds, both personal and collective, ushering us into an era where unity prevails over division, and kindness reigns supreme.

Practicing Unconditional Love

As the rain lightly tapped against the windowpanes, Sony found themselves in a tranquil moment of reflection, piecing together the powerful insights gained on their journey of self-discovery. Unconditional love, a concept that once seemed abstract and elusive, was beginning to crystallize into something tangible, a guiding force that could elevate both individual lives and the collective consciousness of society. It was during one of these quiet evenings, where shadows danced across the walls, and the soft glow of flickering candles created an inviting atmosphere, that they truly began to understand the profound reality of embodying love in daily life. It wasn't just an emotion; it was a practice, an art of living that could lead to transformative change.

In the stillness of that moment, Sony recalled their conversation with the Mentor, a wise being who had illuminated the way forward. "To embody love," they had said, "is to make the conscious choice to rise above the circumstances of your life and the chaos of the world around you." This meant embracing a mindset of compassion, understanding that every person is navigating their own struggles, battles, and heartaches. The realization dawned upon her that each interaction presented an opportunity to choose love over fear, kindness over judgment. With this newfound clarity, they began to observe their surroundings with fresh eyes. A simple encounter at the local market transformed into a chance to connect deeply with the cashier, a woman whose weary eyes told a story of exhaustion. Rather than just grumble about the long line, Sony chose to engage, asking about her day, listening with intent, and exchanging smiles that held a spark of genuine connection. This shift not only brightened the cashier's day but filled her with a sense of warmth, an abiding reminder of the power of love to transcend the mundane.

Every single day became an invitation to practice love in the little things: the way they greeted neighbors, the patience they extended while driving through traffic, the kindness shown to the barista who always went the extra mile. It was not about grand gestures or monumental changes but rather consistent small acts that collectively elevated the energy of those around them. She discovered that the more they practiced these expressions of love, the more the world around them began to reflect that same vibrancy back. Relationships blossomed, trust was built, and previously mundane interactions transformed into something sacred and nourishing. Love, they learned, was the bridge that could mend divisions and heal the wounds of past grievances.

Conversations became a sacred practice in themselves. Forging connections that felt more like reunions of kindred spirits rather than mere exchanges of words offered another avenue to deepen their embodiment of love. Listening actively became an essential part of each interaction, allowing Sony not only to hear words but to connect with emotions, thoughts, and hidden fears. During these shared moments, they embraced vulnerability, recognizing that revealing one's true self is an invitation for others to do the same. A friend confided in them one evening about a personal struggle, and instead of offering solutions, she simply sat in silent understanding, holding space for their friend to express their heart. This exchange encapsulated the essence of unconditional love—the willingness to embrace another's pain without the subtleties of judgment or the compulsion to fix, instead simply being present in the moment and honoring the truth of their experience.

As days morphed into weeks, Sony deliberately sought opportunities to infuse love into the community around them, recognizing the ripple effect it could create not only within their personal circle but extending outwards to strangers. Volunteering at local shelters and welfare organizations became a meaningful endeavor, where they engaged with individuals facing hardship. Each shared smile, each moment of connection, reminded them that unconditional love transcended direct relationships; it was about seeing the divine spark in every soul. Each act became infused with intention, whether it was offering a warm meal, lending a listening ear, or simply extending a smile to someone who might feel invisible in a bustling world. Sony realized how easy it was to slip into the narrative of "them versus us", forgetting that we are all intertwined in a grand tapestry of existence, frayed edges and all, deserving of love and compassion.

Within this community service, they learned another powerful lesson—love is not only about compassion but also about standing in solidarity with those who suffer. Unconditional love encompassed the call to action inspired by love's energy, where speaking up against injustice became intertwined with compassion. With each voice raised in unity, Sony discovered the potency of collective consciousness, the tangible energy generated when individuals unite in a shared vision for a better world. They were reminded that love carries the essence of justice and empathy, where being an ally means lending one's voice where others have been silenced. Understanding that everyone carries burdens unseen became an awakening; it nurtured empathy and heightened their sense of responsibility towards the world, encouraging them to translate love into advocacy, action, and service.

This ongoing journey necessitated actively dismantling the layers of fear, ego, and expectation entrenched in society. The notion became increasingly clear that unconditional love begins with oneself. Inward reflection became non-negotiable. This meant acknowledging past mistakes, forgiving oneself, and embracing imperfect humanity. Loving oneself fully—flaws and all—was the first step in radiating that energy outwardly. Sony took time each day to meditate, taking moments to honor their journey, reflecting on both victories and struggles. Each moment of self-love magnified their capacity to love others, as they learned the importance of filling their own cup before reaching out to fill others'. In embracing their journey with full acceptance, a wave of confidence blossomed, allowing them to embody love as an authentic expression rather than an obligation.

The transformational power of embodying love also prompted her to realign their choices and priorities with their core values. Conversations shifted to discovering deeper connections rather than dabbling in superficial notes. Engaging with literature that spoke to the heart, listening to uplifting music, and surrounding themselves with individuals who reflected the energy they sought to radiate started to shape their reality. Each decision anchored them in a loving mindset, allowing them to weave the threads of love into the very fabric of their day. They began to seek joy actively, recognizing that in celebrating even the smallest moments of beauty—like the arrival of spring flowers or the laughter of children playing—love flourished.

As she mastered the practice of embodying love, they felt a shift not only within themselves but also began to witness a transformation in those around them. It was enchanting to observe the tenderness in relationships flourish, previously tired expressions coming alive with hope, and energy bubbling forth in unexpected gatherings. The focus of their existence shifted toward shared moments, not in the pursuit of self, but in collective joy. This, they found, is where love might truly ignite the flame of hope. It illuminated paths once hidden, formed connections beyond comprehension, and danced in the hearts of those ready to embrace a new way of being.

Ultimately, the strength of unconditional love indicated that the journey forward was not a solitary endeavor. Rather, it became a communal quest, leading to a resounding invitation for everyone to engage in this sacred dance of love together. Each act of love done in pure intention echoed outwards, catalyzing ripples of change that reached far beyond the moments they created. She could envision the blossoming of a harmonious Earth, where all souls played their part, driven by love and purpose, building toward a world where each heart beats in unison, creating a symphony of love that resonates through the ages. The understanding of love evolved into a continuous interplay of giving and receiving, nurturing not just individual healing but awakening a collective spirit eager for transformation. It dawned on them that love is indeed a transformative power, a luminous force directed toward the co-creation of a golden age rooted in understanding, unity, and peace, a journey that started in their heart and extended infinitely outward.

Unity in Diversity

The Beauty of Differences

In the early hours of dawn, as the first rays of sunlight brushed through the clouds, she found themselves entwined in a profound reverie—a moment of introspection that beckoned them into the depths of their consciousness. It was within the embrace of nature, among the rustling leaves and delicate blooms, that they felt compelled to reflect on a truth that resonated at the very core of their being: the beauty of differences. With every heartbeat of the Earth, they realized that life's richness was woven from the vibrancy of diversity, a tapestry where each thread, with its unique color and texture, contributed to the greater narrative of existence. Unity, they mused, is not a mere blending of souls into homogeneity; it is a harmonious symphony composed of distinct notes, each with its own melody that together creates an awe-inspiring chorus.

As Sony observed the world around them, they began to see how the variety of human experiences—shaped by culture, belief, and personal narratives—could lead to deeper understanding and enhanced compassion. Each individual, no matter their background, carried within them the seeds of wisdom, lessons learned through trials and triumphs, akin to constellations adorning the night sky. It was only through the act of genuinely listening and embracing these differences that one could begin to peel back the layers of misunderstanding that often concealed the shared humanity at the core. They recalled their own encounters with people from diverse walks of life. Each meeting was not only an exchange of words but an opportunity to witness the universe reflecting its myriad forms; the passion of an artist, the tranquility of a monk, the resilience of an activist—all contributing to a collective dialogue that enriched their own spirit.

In pondering the significance of diversity, she envisioned a world where people embraced their uniqueness as a source of strength rather than division. They recognized how societal frameworks often cultivated a mindset that favored conformity over individuality, causing rifts that hindered true connection. They had previously floated within the tides of societal expectations, feeling pressured to mold themselves into shapes defined by external validation.

But now, enlightened by their twin flame bond and spiritual journey, they understood the transformative power of living authentically—of allowing their differences to shine. It was an awakening that transcended the self, sparking an understanding of how embodying one's true nature could inspire others to do the same.

With an increasingly enthusiastic heart, she began to envision gatherings of souls, vibrant and diverse, coming together in celebration of their differences. These communal experiences, they realized, had the power to foster a shared consciousness, a collective heartbeat resonating with love and acceptance. They imagined spaces where individuals could share their stories, acknowledging the vastness of existence and the beauty therein. Moments of vulnerability would merge with dialogues of honor, empowering each individual to voice their truths and feelings, chipping away at the invisible walls built by preconceived notions and biases. In actively participating in this sacred communion, they felt a shared mission emerging—a purpose not just for the individual but for the collective.

They recalled conversations that had indelibly etched themselves in their memory; a wise mentor once had shared a simple yet profound phrase: "There is strength in diversity, and love blooms when differences are nurtured." It resonated deeply, revealing itself as the key to unlocking harmony within communities. She understood that determining to embrace each person's unique perspectives would foster a sense of belonging—a sanctuary where everyone felt valued. It was as if flowers in a garden elaborately painted the earth, radiating fragrances that, when harmonized, created a symphony of scents. Such was the essence of humanity! Each aroma, reminiscent of an individual's journey, combined to envelope the world in an intoxicating embrace of understanding.

Returning to the vision of this newly awakened society, they imagined educational spaces as dynamic hubs brimming with opportunity—the radiance of creativity and innovation ignited as students learned not merely from textbooks but through the experiences and contributions of their peers. Lessons woven with authenticity would become the foundation of knowledge, creating empathetic individuals who would step into the world not merely as workers but as stewards of compassion, embracing fellow travelers on this wondrous journey of life. They envisioned diverse teaching methods that catered to varied learning styles, integrating art, music, philosophy, and science as ways of exploring the richness of different cultures and ideas, inspiring students to appreciate and honor the multifaceted kaleidoscope of existence.

In moments of contemplation regarding the impact of collective consciousness on a global scale, she was reminded of the ripple effect—how one courageous choice to honor diversity could alter the course of human destiny. Like water reaching for every crevice within a riverbed, love and compassion would diffuse outward when nurtured through unity. They imagined movements that celebrated authenticity; compassionate activism encompassing the voices of the unheard, rooting for justice, and dignity for those often marginalized by the system. Such endeavors would emerge not solely from passionate individuals but from crowds woven together by their inherent acknowledgment of one another's value—a beautiful manifestation of humanity thriving within shared purpose and respect.

As twilight settled and the moon illuminated the sky, she sensed it was time to share their reflections with like-minded souls who craved change and understanding. They envisioned workshops and gatherings to foster dialogue, inviting hearts and minds to engage openly. The realization that the journey of acceptance is both personal and collective propelled them forward; each individual would illuminate pathways for another, thereby igniting sparks of understanding and compassion across interconnected lives. It was a self-perpetuating cycle—a whirling dance of energies advancing toward a shared future, where love entwined with diversity could thrive without restraint.

Addressing their community, they felt the need to remind each soul present of the inherent beauty rooted within every individual: "We are like the colors of an artist's palette. The reds, blues, and yellows find themselves otherwise mundane if not blended with the others' essence. Together, we can paint a masterpiece—an extravagant mural of our existence where every stroke of diversity counts." It was a charged moment as they spoke, realizing that nourishing unity found its expression in acknowledging each person's unique essence, allowing that very essence to dance freely, unfettered by societal norms. In those moments, their heart stirred with hope—the epicenter of dreams for a new Earth, shimmering with the luminosity of love, echoed with the reverberations of countless voices proclaiming, "We are different, and in embracing this difference, we shall become truly one."

From that moment forward, Sony felt propelled by inspiration, knowing they carried a sacred flame within them that could illuminate paths for others, drawing them toward understanding and compassion. They understood that while change may stem from individual journeys, it was through unity that the ripples would expand, carrying the message of acceptance across the globe. The significance of embracing the beauty of differences was not merely an act of kindness but a revolutionary step towards restoring balance to a world thirsting for love. Together, they could envision a New Earth—a sanctuary where individual stories were celebrated, and every soul found its place within the divine spectrum of existence. As the first stars emerged in the night sky, she cast their dreams outward, reaching for an existence intertwined with love, embracing the vastness of the human experience as they embarked on a journey toward unity, compassion, and an unwavering belief in a brighter tomorrow

Building Bridges

As the raindrops danced gracefully against the window, she felt an awakening stir within the depths of their soul—a longing to build bridges between people, to forge connections that transcended the ego-driven divides so prominent in the world. The serene beauty of nature in that moment seemed to whisper secrets of unity. She understood that the true essence of humanity lay not in the separation of identities and cultures, but rather in the rich tapestry woven from the threads of unique experiences, each one adding texture and depth to the greater whole. This realization was not merely a fleeting thought, but a profound truth that resonated with the frequency of love, an energy that had the power to melt away the barriers that confined human hearts.

In their musings, she recalled the myriad occasions where misunderstanding had bred resentment and division. They remembered conversations with those who held contrasting beliefs—how often had egos clashed, masking the shared values beneath? Sony envisioned a world where dialogue was infused with empathy, where ears and hearts were open to hear not just the words spoken, but the emotions that stirred beneath them. To create real connections, they knew it was essential to guide others to this understanding, to encourage a departure from the defensive stances of debate, and to nurture an environment where vulnerability was welcomed with open arms. They began to see that bridging divides rested on the willingness to acknowledge differences while also celebrating them as gifts that could enrich the collective experience.

One vision that came to her during a meditative moment was a grand tapestry hanging in the sacred space of their heart. Each thread represented a person, a culture, a belief, uniquely vibrant and essential to the canvas of life. They felt an exhilarating urgency to share this vision with others, to invite them to weave their threads into the tapestry that connected them all. The mantra of unity beckoned—there was beauty in the diversity of thought and experience, an understanding that each individual was a vital part of the larger whole. They began to ponder various ways to nurture these connections, igniting a movement rooted in harmony and acceptance that would ripple throughout the community and beyond.

A profound opportunity came in the form of community gatherings, which she envisioned as collective spaces for sharing wisdom and building relationships. They dreamed of hosting events that would encourage storytelling, inviting individuals to recount their journeys—the struggles they faced, the triumphs they celebrated, and the love that illuminated their paths. In creating a welcoming environment, Sony aimed to facilitate genuine conversations that would draw out the common threads of humanity found in every story, allowing attendees to relate to each other on a deeply personal level, fostering understanding and cultivating compassion. They realized the importance of celebrating each person's narrative while highlighting the universal lessons of love and resilience that connected them all.

However, she understood that sharing stories was just one element of bridge-building; they also needed to create spaces for collaborative action. They envisioned workshops where diverse groups could come together to tackle pressing community issues, engaging in dialogue that was led not by competing agendas but by a collective desire to uplift and serve. This format could break down the barriers of mistrust and prejudice, inviting participants to glimpse the unique perspectives and experiences of others. Sony wanted to create projects that not only reaffirmed individual identities but also illuminated broader societal issues, nurturing a sense of responsibility towards one another. In witnessing the power of collaboration, participants could bond over shared goals that helped them transcend their differences, fostering a unity anchored in purpose.

In this reflection, Sony realized that the role of a bridge-builder extended beyond inviting others to come together; it also involved actively working to dismantle the obstacles that prevented reconciliation. They identified the importance of addressing misconceptions and stereotypes, recognizing the subtle ways in which societal narratives perpetuated division. They felt a gnawing responsibility to challenge these mindsets, to be a voice that encouraged mindful awareness. An important aspect would involve organizing dialogues open to all walks of life, where differing opinions could coexist without animosity. Together, participants could explore uncomfortable topics, providing a safe space for questions and discussions that would empower them to break down the walls they had built around their hearts.

As the rain poured heavier outside, she sensed that this journey was about transforming perceptions, planting seeds of empathy where fear and ignorance had previously taken root. They envisioned nurturing these seeds through acts of kindness, small gestures that rippled outward, ultimately cultivating a garden of compassion within their community. They planned to organize volunteer opportunities, encouraging individuals from all backgrounds to contribute to causes that served their shared humanity—soup kitchens, mentorship programs, environmental clean-ups. These invitations would foster connection through collaboration, demonstrating that the act of giving drew people together, weaving intricate bonds of kindness that flourished amidst life's complexities.

In musing about the importance of unity, she couldn't overlook the bond they shared with their twin flame. This spiritual connection served as a beacon, a model of unconditional love and support that transcended limitations, speaking to the very core of human potential. Recognizing the reciprocal relationship between individual wholeness and collective unity, they pondered how radiant relationships inspired transformative ripple effects within communities. Every interaction held the potential to awaken hidden depths of understanding, and through mutual growth, they could foster a sense of oneness that enveloped all beings. Sony recognized their twin flame's journey alongside them as a source of hope, offering a template for building bridges through the exuding energy of love that allowed them to find strength in life's trials.

As Sony flowed through the landscapes of their contemplations, they became aware that the bridge-building process was an ongoing evolution—an invitation to remain open to the dynamic nature of human connection, one that demanded patience, vulnerability, and persistence. They embraced the idea that not every encounter would lead to profound understanding; sometimes, it would require navigating challenges and navigating discomfort. Yet, they felt resolute in their purpose, driven by the commitment to invite compassion into the world every day, to share their vision and practice the principles of acceptance, benediction, and integration. Each small step toward outreach contributed to a greater momentum, as if the universe itself conspired to align them with others who shared the same vision of creating a harmonious Earth.

Ultimately, Sony recognized that the process of building bridges necessitated a delicate balance between self-discovery and collective growth—where they could never forget the importance of their own journey, of nurturing their spirit while simultaneously fostering connections with others. This dual role as both an individual and a collective being allowed them to embrace the inherent unity of existence. In encouraging compassion, they could empower others to own their sacred dignity and context, and together, they would resonate with the harmonic vibrations of love that floated delicately through the air, perhaps transforming not only their hearts but the world at large.

The vision of a united humanity stood clear in their mind's eye: hands joined together in solidarity, each person's unique pulse contributing to the greater heartbeat of the cosmos—a world awakened to its potential, where love impelled action, and every soul became a lighthouse guiding others toward compassionate understanding. The rain slowed to a gentle drizzle outside, and as the sun began to break through the clouds, a brilliant arc of colors emerged— a reminder that hope exists even in the storm, that bridges can be built with intention, and that love has the power to light the way toward a golden age of understanding.

A Tapestry of Souls

As the rain gently cascaded against the windowpanes, Sony found themselves lost in contemplation, analyzing the intricate tapestry of humanity woven throughout the cosmos. Each thread, a distinct soul pulsating with its own rhythm, color, and vibration; yet, when interlaced with the others, they created a masterpiece—an expansive representation of existence that transcended the individual and echoed the collective. In this moment of serene reflection, they were struck by the profound reality that unity did not diminish individual essence; rather, it enriched the fabric of being, grounding the truth that every soul is interconnected, forming a singular heartbeat that reverberates across the universe. Each person's journey, filled with trials and triumphs, was not an isolated thread; instead, it contributed to a larger story—an intricate tale of love, suffering, enlightenment, and awakening that spanned the ages.

As she marveled at the power of unity, they recalled their own experiences with diversity. Growing up in a multicultural environment, they had been fortunate enough to interact with various beliefs, customs, and perspectives. Each interaction illuminated the richness that diversity brings, sparking curiosity and empathy. They vividly remembered joyous gatherings that celebrated different traditions, where laughter intertwined with the melodies of various tongues—each nuance expressing an unutterable truth about the human experience. Even in moments of disagreement, they witnessed how the dance of perspectives and ideas could lead to deeper understanding and growth. Life became a harmonious intersection where learning flourished. It was a reminder that embracing diversity was not merely an act of tolerance but an essential step toward cultivating compassion and awareness.

She contemplated a crucial facet of unity: vulnerability. In a world often dominated by ego, it was far too easy to fall into the habit of separation, erecting barriers that veiled true connection—and yet within that vulnerability lay the key to transformative unity. When souls dared to shed their defenses and expose their innermost selves, the rich tapestry of existence blossomed into vibrant shades of love and understanding. It became evident that each person's vulnerability served as a bridge, allowing hearts to reach out, to touch one another, to share their stories of hardship and joy alike. They realized that the more one could embrace their authenticity amidst a sea of differences, the more liberating it felt—an invitation to others to do the same. In this shared space of courage, they could inspire others to reveal their vulnerabilities, thus forging bonds that transcended superficial distinctions.

In pondering the greater global tapestry, Sony considered the currents of disconnection and fragmentation that swept across societies. These currents propelled individuals into isolation, where the matrix of control sowed doubt and fear. Many succumbed to the illusion that their opinions and beliefs were the only valid narratives, vying for societal dominance, creating rifts of indifference and hatred in its wake. This was not merely a disservice to the individuals themselves but a disheartening betrayal of humanity's collective growth. They understood that the beautiful complexity of being human is rooted in contrasting perspectives, each deserving of recognition. She yearned to see a world where stories of diverse experiences and backgrounds converged in dialogue rather than conflict. It was only through the acknowledgment and appreciation of these differences that humanity could reach a deeper collective consciousness—an elevation towards unity that embraced the multifaceted essence of existence.

With their minds racing, they turned their thoughts to the elders and mentors who had planted seeds of wisdom in their path. These wise figures had imparted invaluable lessons regarding the power of a compassionate heart, reminding her that empathy nurtured the threads connecting the tapestry of souls. They recalled the community leaders with their remarkable ability to draw forth people from various walks of life, gathering them not to impose ideology, but to foster mutual understanding and support within the community. Activism infused with love and compassion had the power to ignite the flames of change, instilling hope within those who felt lost in the chaos around them. She could sense that this was their calling—to emulate the same spirit of gathering the hearts of the like-minded to create a movement that encouraged healing and understanding between diverse groups.

As the evening progressed, she felt a surge of passion in envisioning their role as a catalyst for transformation. They realized that within the pursuit to cocreate a new harmonious Earth, they had the ability to actively engage others in dialogue that explored unity through diversity. It would require creating spaces—both virtual and physical—where individuals could come together to share their stories, letting go of fear to foster empathy in return. Workshops, discussions, and community gatherings focused on celebrating differences would light the fire of interconnectedness, allowing barriers to dissolve and compassion to flourish. They envisioned a world where art, music, and narratives captivated hearts, inspiring people to appreciate the talents and beauty woven within each unique thread of existence.

With each of these reflections, it became clear to her that every moment held the opportunity to heal and unite. Embracing the diversity of the human experience required not only understanding but also action—an unwavering commitment to encourage and cultivate love among individuals and communities alike. The journey toward a new, harmonious Earth would demand courage, patience, and an openness to listen, absorb, and reflect. It became apparent that change starts within each individual soul, which, when nurtured into awakening, could create ripples of compassion reaching far and wide.

In the grand symmetry that marked this journey, she understood that they were a thread in this ever-evolving tapestry—a thread that could nourish the fabric of humanity through love, empathy, and gratitude. Each interaction held the potential to change someone's life, to awaken dormant possibilities, and to grow a connection that transcended superficial differences. Every heartfelt conversation spoken in kindness could create waves of change that traveled beyond the confines of the individual soul. It was through engagement, unity, and the embrace of diversity that the propagation of love could reshape the essence of humanity, leading to a more profound understanding of the sacred connection shared among all beings.

As the rainfall slowly subsided, revealing the crispness of a new dawn, she felt an invigorating surge of hope and purpose. They recognized the fortitudes within them and others, the ability to rise together, hand-in-hand, into this expansive reality of interconnectedness. With their heart full of resolve, they were ready to embark on the next phase of their journey—continuously championing the movement that beckoned a rising of sacred souls towards a new harmonious Earth.

The Role of Empathy

Empathy Defined

In the tranquil embrace of nature, where the gentle murmur of leaves danced in rhythm with the soft patter of rain, Sony found themselves contemplating the profound nature of empathy. Surrounded by the lushness of the world, they felt an awakening within — a stirring sense that empathy was not merely an emotion but a pivotal force, capable of creating infinite connections among souls. In their reflections, they began to unravel the layers of this formidable trait, understanding that it transcended mere sympathy or compassion. Empathy, they realized, was about plunging into the depths of another's experience, feeling their joys and sorrows, triumphs and despair, almost as if walking alongside them on their unique paths.

As the realization dawned, Sony began to see empathy as the antidote to the prevailing isolation permeating society. In a world often segmented by divisive beliefs and rigid judgments, empathy had the power to dissolve the barriers erected by misunderstanding. It served as a bridge, spanning the chasms that separated one individual from another, allowing for richer and deeper connections. They envisioned people standing on opposite sides of a divide, armed with their own narratives, insecurities, and fears, and it became clear to them that empathy could offer a pathway to understanding. Instead of analyzing and labeling one another from the safe distance of predetermined assumptions, human beings could, through the practice of empathy, step into each other's shoes and see the world through their eyes — an awakening of sorts that beckoned to be pursued.

As they meandered through these ponderings, she recognized that the journey toward a harmonious Earth demanded more than just individual enlightenment; it necessitated the collective embrace of empathy. Within the sacred journey of twin flames, where love ignited and transformed souls, empathy became the common thread interwoven with their experiences. Twin flames, as they invoked remembrance within one another, found clarity in their connection as they navigated the waves of humanity together. Her thoughts drifted to how twin flames, often seen as mirrors reflecting each other's strengths and vulnerabilities, could harness the essence of empathy as a tool for elevation, not only for themselves but for the collective consciousness of the world around them.

Empathy, they observed, had the ability to heal wounds both seen and unseen. The countless stories and struggles that filled the hearts of those around them came alive in their vivid imaginings. The homeless man sitting quietly on the pavement, drenched in the rain and despair, held an entire universe of pain within his existence. The woman in the café, furrowed brow and trembling hands as she processed her impending loss, represented countless individuals grappling with grief and uncertainty. Each person, each story held a sacred lesson, and the key to unlocking that treasure trove of wisdom lay in the embrace of empathy, allowing for impeccable interconnection. In each shared breath and weight of sorrow held by another, she felt the spirit of unity whispering, a gentle reminder that every soul traversed an intricate web of experiences.

They delved deeper, uncovering how empathy acted as a catalyst for understanding and compassion. This divine connection could ignite a fire within the hearts of individuals, propelling them to act in the service of one another. If one dared to engage deeply in empathetic listening, the resonance of shared human experience would blossom into cooperative action. Beyond mere words of support, empathy inspired individuals to extend their hands toward those in need, to engage in acts of kindness that fostered a sense of belonging. She imagined communities transformed through the lens of empathy, where discussions replaced arguments, understanding overshadowed judgment, and unity reigned in place of division.

Recognizing that empathy required practice and intent, Sony encountered a pivotal moment of clarity. Empathy flourishes when nurtured, and to tap into this divine wellspring would require not only awareness but bold action. They began to ponder ways to cultivate an empathetic spirit. How could they encourage others to value the narratives of those different from themselves? How could they develop a community steeped in understanding, where everyone was reminded of their interdependency and sacred individuality? As they reflected upon these questions, they felt a resolve form within them, a whispering promise that the journey of empathy could be the antidote to the chaos so prevalent in the world.

In their exploration of this powerful force, Sony sought wisdom from mentors and kindred spirits who had traversed similar paths. Gathering in circles of seekers, where stories flowed as freely as the river's currents, they initiated discussions that opened hearts and minds. Together, they unwrapped the intricate layers of empathy, dissecting its traits and impact, correlating personal experiences with universal truths, validating the voices of the unheard, and reaffirming the beauty of diverse narratives. Through these interactions, she witnessed the miraculous transformation that occurred as the seeds of empathy took root, creating blossoming friendships, understanding relationships, and a profound alliance toward shared goals.

Amidst the enlightening gatherings, a profound truth began to reveal itself — empathy was not just a lofty ideal; it was a foundational principle necessary for the evolution of humanity. The inquiries swirled within their mind: What if empathy became a guiding doctrine in every facet of life? What if political leaders, educators, and individuals in positions of power committed sincerely to roping empathy into their heartfelt actions? Would institutions forged in greed and ambition yield to communities centered around collective flourishing? She envisioned a world where policies are constructed not only with intellect but with compassion, deeply cognizant of the lives they would impact.

As she embraced the mystical beauty of empathy, they began to nurture not only their understanding but also their application of it; life became enriched through interactions that were grounded in the shared human experience. They made a conscious effort to break through their own fears of vulnerability, allowing others to witness their authentic selves. In sharing their vulnerabilities, they extended an invitation for reciprocity — an open-hearted embrace of honesty, where the staying power of compassion could elevate conversations into realms previously untapped. It was here, in this sacred exchange, that they could witness the healing nature of empathy manifesting, touching hearts, and stimulating awakening on profound levels.

With each encounter and each conversation, Sony carried empathy forward, feeling the transformative power ripple through their community.

Spurred on by a desire to awaken the slumbering hearts around them, they initiated communal gatherings where stories were shared, expressed through art and creativity — gatherings infused with the essence of compassion. Through music, dance, and spoken word, individuals came together to weave their narratives into a vibrant tapestry, resonating with the truths that bind humanity together. Each gathering offered a sanctuary of understanding, a place where people could express their worries, joys, and dreams, immersed in collective vulnerability that unfurled a beautiful canvas of support.

Slowly, Sony saw that this practice of empathy bore ripe fruits — a blossoming community characterized by mutual respect, compassion, and support. The societal fabric transformed, allowing the possible evidence of a new Earth piercing its way through the cracks of the old. It was a world where empathy reigned, and every soul became a beacon of light for others. She recognized with clarity that empathy, once harnessed, had grandeur within its simplicity — a magnificent truth that could alter the trajectory of humanity itself.

As they continued this journey of understanding and application, she dove headfirst into embracing the essence of empathy, recognizing its sacredness in unlocking potential. Each challenge that arose became an opportunity to practice empathy, to extend the moral courage to dig deeper into uncomfortable spaces, both within themselves and within others. They reached out with heartfelt compassion to the disenfranchised and the marginalized, realizing that when empathy was woven into humanity's collective consciousness, it fortified the foundation upon which hope, love, and transformation could flourish.

Through tireless exploration and active practice, she began to awaken not only the consciousness of those surrounding them but also their own. They felt gratitude swell in their heart as they recognized the beauty of this journey; empathy became their guiding compass. It illuminated every interaction and inspired them to create ripples of compassion that danced across communities. She envisioned the tremendous potential that could arise when empathy was given space to breathe and shine, knowing now, irrevocably, that they stood on the threshold of a new Earth, one where empathy could usher in a golden age of love, connection, and profound understanding.

Empathy in Action

On this transformative journey towards a new harmonious Earth, Sony comes to understand that empathy is not merely an abstract ideal to be admired from a distance but a profound and active practice that can reshape lives and communities. As they reflect on encounters with others—friends, family, even strangers—they recognize that empathy often extends beyond the confines of mere sympathy; it resonates with the essence of shared humanity. Realizing its significance, they begin to explore how empathy can serve as a bridge that connects individuals and fosters understanding amidst a chaotic world fraught with division. She learns that to embody empathy is to step into another's shoes, to embrace their experiences, feelings, and perspectives, allowing for a deeper connection with their stories and struggles. It is through this immersion that true understanding blossoms, transforming the isolation into camaraderie and healing the rifts that separate souls from one another.

Through personal experiences, Sony witnesses the transformative power of empathy, especially in moments when individuals feel misunderstood or alienated. In their mind, a potent memory surfaces—a stark encounter with a community member who had faced prejudice and discrimination. They had noticed the tension in the air when the person spoke about their struggles, the defensiveness leaping from the very words uttered. But instead of glossing over the uncomfortable feelings, she bravely engaged in dialogue, even when uncertainty loomed. In that moment, as they listened deeply, they chose not to react defensively or dismissively; instead, they allowed the vulnerable emotions shared to wash over them like a gentle tide. They felt the anger, the hurt, and the yearning for acceptance, and it ignited a deep desire within her to act—not merely with understanding but with compassion and determination.

Driven by this revelation, she explores how empathy can be made manifest in everyday interactions, thus setting about implementing small but meaningful acts that ripple out into the larger community. They begin with simple gestures: offering a listening ear to those who feel unheard, volunteering their time to support the most vulnerable, and advocating for those who lack a voice in the larger societal narrative. Each act of engagement becomes a cornerstone of transformation, revealing how powerfully empathy can catalyze action, allowing feelings of disconnection to give way to tangible expressions of care and support. By deliberately placing empathy at the forefront of their interactions, she fosters a culture that values understanding, ensuring that every individual feels seen and valued, irrespective of their background or beliefs.

Sony recognizes that empathy must also extend into the political and social realms, motivating them to engage in community outreach. They envision spaces where individuals can come together to share their stories, engage in dialogue, and cultivate understanding. They organize workshops, inviting diverse voices to participate, creating platforms for the sharing of lived experiences that highlight the unique struggles and triumphs faced within the community. As participants begin to share their narratives, she witnesses the emergence of a collective consciousness—an awakening to the common threads that connect the participants far beyond their perceived differences. Moments of laughter and tears weave through those gatherings, creating a tapestry rich in empathy, connection, and mutual healing, as individuals begin to recognize not only their struggles but the shared hopes they hold for a brighter future.

The power of empathy also becomes evident as she encourages their community to adopt new perspectives that illuminate the importance of inclusivity. By hosting dialogue sessions centered on the challenges faced by marginalized groups, they evoke an atmosphere of respectful curiosity that invites all participants to reflect on their biases. This creates a safe space for collective introspection where discomfort is acknowledged without judgment, allowing participants to confront their assumptions head-on. She serves as a guide in these discussions, translating complex emotions into relatable experiences, reminding everyone present of their inherent interconnectedness. They reinforce the idea that each person's story matters and that every single voice contributes remarkably towards the healing of divisions, ultimately fostering an environment of unity and collaboration.

In time, community members begin to embody empathy in their daily lives, recognizing its transformative potential in shaping their interactions with each other and the world around them. A chain reaction emerges, as family members support one another in their respective challenges, neighbors initiate honest conversations about their differences, and local businesses pledge to adopt ethical practices centered on compassion. Sony feels an exhilarating sense of purpose, watching with joy as those around them begin to understand that empathy is not just a response to suffering; it is the balm that soothes the wounds of division and the catalyst that propels them toward collective growth and understanding. Each genuine interaction serves as a building block, laying the foundation for a more compassionate society, reflecting a brighter vision of the new harmonious Earth they are tirelessly working to co-create.

Harnessing the energy of their community efforts, she delves deeper into empathy's role in reconciliation and healing. They seek out experts and mentors who can shed light on the science of empathy and the steps one can take to nurture it further within their environment. They learn of various practices—active listening, non-violent communication, and mindfulness techniques—that serve to deepen one's capacity for empathy. Armed with this newfound knowledge, she synthesizes these practices, sharing them during community gatherings, igniting a sacred dialogue dedicated to not only addressing pain but also fostering resilience and the power to thrive amidst adversity.

One poignant moment remains etched in Sony's heart—a gathering that witnessed a heart-wrenching story of an individual who had twice experienced the harsh realities of loss and betrayal. This person had built walls around their heart, reluctant to reach out and form connections with others. When they finally spoke, everyone's attention was drawn toward them, the room enveloped in an intimate stillness. Sony, sensing an opportunity for empathy, gently guided the group into a supportive embrace, encouraging others to speak their truth and offer love to the storyteller. As voices intertwined, narratives echoed within that sacred space, forming a web of love and understanding that tenderly reminded each participant of the inherent resilience they carried and the strength they drew from unity. In that moment, barriers crumbled, and the air itself grew lighter, filled with newfound hope.

She realizes that embodying empathy does not mean becoming a martyr or sacrificing oneself; rather, it means creating an equilibrium where self-care and altruism coexist harmoniously. By prioritizing their emotional health, they can sustainably spread this message of love, compassion, and understanding. They encourage community members to reflect on their well-being, urging them to engage in practices that nurture their mental and emotional fulfillment. This reciprocity fosters a culture where individuals empower one another, thus creating a resilient support network that acknowledges the importance of collective health while prioritizing personal growth.

The notion of empathy as an active and change-making force solidifies within Sony's heart, becoming a beacon that leads them onward. They undertake an initiative to partner with local organizations to launch campaigns for mental health awareness and emotional support, inviting external voices into the community to address the lack of resources and stigma around vulnerability. This collaborative effort strengthens the community and ripples outward, creating dialogues around empathy that resonate far beyond geographical boundaries. They witness individuals from various walks of life unite toward common goals, embracing their unique strengths and perspectives to embolden their collective mission.

As they stand amidst the vibrant tapestry of interconnected lives, Sony reflects on the journey of transformation they have undertaken. From the quiet revelations inscribed in their heart on a rainy evening to the magnificent unfolding of a united community striving for empathy and understanding, they feel a pure certainty that deep connections can manifest under adverse circumstances. Each small step taken in embracing empathy as an action underscores the beauty of human resilience. She understands that though the challenges may seem insurmountable at times, the love ignited by empathy can lead to the creation of a new harmonious Earth, where the threads of humanity are beautifully interwoven, unveiling a tapestry rich in compassion, understanding, and unity—a true testament to their sacred journey towards peace and prosperity.

Cultivating Empathy

As the rain pattered softly against the window, Sony sat cross-legged on the floor of their sacred space, the flickering candlelight casting playful shadows across the room. It was here, amidst the scents of wood and herbs, that they began a deeper dive into the essence of empathy, an essential component for bridging the divides that had long separated humanity. They realized that empathy was not merely an emotion; it was a profound and transformative experience that allowed individuals to break away from the chains of indifference and misunderstanding that had bound society for far too long. Embracing empathy would not only enrich their own spiritual journey but also pave the way for a collective awakening, fostering genuine connections based on compassion and love. In that moment of reflection, a series of exercises emerged in their mind, each aiming to deepen their understanding and practice of empathy, while also inviting others to join this enlightening venture.

The first exercise focused on active listening, a powerful means by which one can step outside themselves and fully immerse in another's experience. She envisioned a gathering where individuals would come together to engage in deep conversations. During these exchanges, the participants would take turns sharing their thoughts and emotions while the other displayed their intent listening without interruption, offering only gentle nods of encouragement or validation. This would allow the speaker to feel heard and valued, while the listener would cultivate an awareness of the feelings and experiences that lay beneath the surface of mere words. She understood that often, it was not solely the content of a conversation that mattered but the energy exchanged between individuals. A shared glance, a subtle smile, or the warmth of a receptive heart could illuminate understanding beyond simple dialogue. In embracing this exercise, they imagined the individuals arriving with their burdens and joys, leaving behind a little light in each other's hearts, each transformed as they forged bonds through empathy.

Sony also envisioned another exercise set in nature, a realm where the interconnectedness of all beings was palpable. They would guide a group of seekers to a sprawling field where they would sit in a circle, allowing the sounds of rustling leaves and distant birds to fill the air. The focus of this gathering would be to connect with the earth beneath them and recognize their innate relationship with nature. One by one, participants would be encouraged to share a moment when they felt deeply connected to the natural world— perhaps a vivid memory of the sun warming their skin or the scent of rain-soaked earth. As they listened to each story, participants would be encouraged to visualize the experiences of their fellow seekers, cultivating a sense of unity rather than separation. A profound ripple effect would unfold when they acknowledged that each person was an integral thread in the vast tapestry of life, dispelling feelings of isolation and allowing a sense of belonging to emerge. Experiencing this connection would elevate their consciousness, enhancing the empathy that blossoms naturally between kindred spirits dedicated to awakening.

In a subsequent exercise, the concept of perspective-taking came to life, serving as another way to deepen empathy and understanding. She imagined an immersive role-play scenario where participants would embody the beliefs and experiences of people whose lives differed greatly from their own. Each seeker would pose as someone who faced challenges that were foreign to their own lives. For instance, one might take on the role of a refugee, another that of an elderly individual struggling with a shifting cultural landscape, while yet another could embody a child grappling with the complexities of mental health. The participants would then interact in guided discussions, allowing them to express both their joys and difficulties while fully immersing themselves in the chosen character's essence. It would be a powerful exercise, as participants would come to comprehend not just the narratives of others, but the profound emotions that accompanied those experiences—fear, hope, longing, and resilience. By walking a mile in someone else's shoes, they would soon understand that empathy transcends simply feeling sorry for another; it is experiencing life through another's lens, fostering a deep and abiding connection that would inspire loving action toward those who suffer.

Sony also felt the yearning to incorporate the arts into their journey of empathy, recognizing that creativity often served as a bridge to understanding. They envisioned an artistic workshop where participants could express their feelings and experiences through various mediums—painting, writing, or music—while exploring themes centered around empathy and connection. Each individual would select a prompt that called to their hearts, such as "Write about a time you felt isolated," or "Express what healing looks like for you." Afterwards, they would gather to share their creations. This open expression would encourage participants not just to comprehend one another's stories but to feel them deeply in their bones. The colors of an artwork, the notes of a song, or the cadence of spoken words could evoke emotions that transcend language, allowing the collective heart to resonate with shared experiences, joys, and sorrows. Through the arts, she envisioned a blossoming community where the expressions of vulnerability became a sacred thread that interwove their souls together, fostering compassion and reliance among them.

As their understanding of empathy deepened, she also recognized the need to incubate a spirit of self-compassion within. They knew that while it was essential to extend empathy outwardly to others, it was equally important to cultivate it inwardly. She imagined a reflective exercise where individuals would participate in a meditation focused on self-acceptance. They would sit quietly, eyes closed, breathing deeply as they invited feelings of love and understanding for themselves to flow through each inhalation and exhalation. This would help dissolve the harsh self-judgment that often holds people back from extending genuine empathy to others. She envisioned participants finding themselves confronting their own wounds, deeply acknowledging and accepting every part of themselves, even the imperfections they once sought to hide. By nurturing themselves through this practice of self-compassion, they would eventually cultivate a reservoir of kindness that could easily overflow into their interactions with others. Fostering love within would empower them to uplift and connect with those around them in a way that fostered healing within the collective.

In weaving together these exercises of empathy, Sony understood that the journey toward a new harmonious Earth began with each individual's willingness to step beyond the suffocating confines of ego. Empathy, they concluded, was a sacred mandate and a doorway to connection, healing, and transformation. By acknowledging the shared humanity in one another, they were instrumental in creating a ripple effect of compassion—one that refused to be eradicated by the prevailing chaos of the world. As she fervently envisioned these exercises taking shape within their community, their heart swelled with hope. People would gather, breaking bread, laughing, crying, sharing life stories, creating threads of interconnectedness that would blanket their surroundings, igniting a potent movement grounded in love and understanding. They could already sense the seeds of empathy being sown, knowing that they would usher forth a new era of cooperation, love, and unity that transcended the boundaries that had long divided humanity.

With a steadfast resolve resonating through their being, they set intentions for these exercises, feeling the warmth of divine support wrap around them. A growing realization surfaced that empathy was not just a personal venture; it was a collective mission to weave together the very fabric of existence into something beautiful and harmonious. As the candle flickered, casting ambient light over the room, she smiled, feeling grateful that the journey to cultivate empathy was both a gift and a responsibility they were willing to embrace with an open heart. The transformations that awaited were not confined to merely their story; they would echo across communities and generations, inviting others to join in the ongoing process of awakening. This journey was only just beginning, and the prospect of rising together into a new harmonious Earth shimmered brightly in their heart and mind as they prepared to share these sacred teachings with those willing to walk the path of love and connection.

The Journey of Co-Creation

Co-Creating with the Universe

As the rain continued to fall lightly outside, casting a soft melody that intertwined with the rhythmic beat of Sony's heart, a new awareness blossomed within. It was a revelation akin to the sudden warming embrace of the sun breaking through a dense layer of clouds, illuminating the world with its vibrant energy. This inner awakening was the understanding of co-creation—a profound realization that the universe is not a distant observer of our lives, but an active participant, inviting them to play a vital role in the weaving of their own reality. This moment didn't simply give way to clarity; it allowed them to see the threads of their existence, each one vibrating with potential and possibility, waiting patiently to be pulled into a grand tapestry of divine manifestation.

While contemplating the powerful co-creative energy that surrounded them, Sony recalled a conversation with their mentor, a wise figure who had opened their eyes to the mysteries of the universe and the intricate dance of creation. With a warm, knowing smile, the mentor had often spoken of the cosmos as a living organism—not merely a vast expanse of stars, but a vivid expression of consciousness. "We are not just beings navigating through life," they would often say. "We are participants in an ever-unfolding cosmic play, where every thought, action, and intention ripples through the fabric of existence." This perspective shifted her understanding of their life's path, allowing them to embrace the idea that they were not bound to the dictates of fate; rather, they held the power to influence their own trajectory.

Sony began to realize that co-creation was about more than simply wishing for change; it was about aligning themselves with the vibrational frequency of the universe. It entailed a commitment to stepping into their role as an instrument of change, allowing the divine energy to flow through them, unencumbered by limitations of doubt or fear. Images of the interconnectedness of all beings played out in their mind, painting a picture of unity, the universe, and the soul. They could feel it—the infinite possibility that lay at their fingertips— waiting to manifest through surrendered intention and heartfelt desire. The act of co-creation is a symphony where each note represents their unique essence, contributing to the harmonious expression of life.

In the moments of stillness that followed, Sony closed their eyes and envisioned a new world; a new Earth awash in love and compassion, free from the confines of hate and division. They understood that this vision was not just a fleeting dream, but rather a call to action driven by the profound connection they had with the universe. The intricate balance of nature mirrored their feelings; just as the earth and sky danced together, so too could they dance in tandem with the divine. In this sacred partnership, intentions were the seeds planted in the fertile soil of their spirit; with nurturing love, these seeds would inevitably bloom into the reality they sought to manifest.

In practical terms, co-creation demanded a set of conscious choices, beginning with the purification of thoughts and intentions. She recognized that a fundamental aspect of this process was their willingness to release the ego's grip. Ego often served as a detriment, proposing limiting beliefs that created barriers between themselves and the divine flow. With every passing moment of contemplation, they felt a wave of encouragement wash over them, inviting them to anchor themselves firmly in the heart space of love and gratitude. The divine could be trusted to weave their intentions into the greater fabric of life, providing clarity and purpose to each inspired step taken in conscious awareness. When ego fell away, what remained was the authentic self—the part of them that intimately understood their innate power as a co-creator.

Emboldened by this knowing, Sony began to actively engage in practices that fostered their relationship with the divine. Meditation became a sacred ritual, a bridge connecting their being with the universe, where they could listen to the whispers of inspirations and insights that guided their path. During these moments of stillness, they found themselves surrounded by the loving embrace of the divine presence, an entity that echoed reassurance and support. With each session, they learned to trust their intuition, the subtle nudges from the cosmos guiding their decisions toward opportunities that aligned with their desires.

Connection with like-minded souls emerged as another significant component of this co-creative journey. There was something undeniably powerful about gathering with those who shared a mutual vision of transformation; it amplified intentions and ignited the fire of possibility. Every gathering was a beautiful affirmation of their shared essence, showcasing the strength that manifests when hearts unite. Together, they began to weave a new narrative, one rich with love and hope, reflecting their innate brilliance as sacred beings on a mission to change the world.

Among these gatherings, celebrations blossomed—moments where collective energy surged, and intentions seemed to leap into existence with astonishing ease. It was during one of these events that Sony felt an undeniable current coursing through the collective heart; they were no longer just individual souls operating in isolation but a chorus of voices harmonizing together. The unity resonated deeply within them, illuminating a path forward soaked in purpose and inexhaustible potential. In these beautiful moments, they felt the presence of the divine enveloping them, affirming that they were indeed co-creating a legacy of love.

The road ahead was not without its challenges. Sony often faced skepticism, both from the outside world and within themselves, creating ripples of doubt that threatened to undermine their newfound commitment. Yet, with each passing trial, they would return to their breath, center themselves in love, and embrace the lessons inherent in the struggle. They understood by now that every experience was an invitation to rise, an opportunity for growth and transformation. Each seemingly insurmountable obstacle became a chance to reaffirm their connection with the universe, an opportunity to manifest resilience born from the depths of their sacred essence.

As they emerged stronger from each of these experiences, a sense of urgency took hold. The realization that time was both fluid and finite propelled them to embody the tenets of co-creation more fiercely. The world outside was changing; waves of awakening surged through the collective consciousness, and so many souls were on the precipice of recognizing their own divine power. She began to see themselves not just as a participant in this transformative uprising, but as a catalyst for change, igniting sparks of awakening in those around them. Each interaction became a chance to explore the magic of possibility and inspire others to embrace their role as co-creators alongside the universe.

And so, the journey transformed into an ongoing dialogue between themselves and the cosmos, a sacred exchange that continually birthed new ideas and projects aimed at nurturing collective coherence. Attempts to bring the community together took shape as grand events that showcased love and compassion—from gathering for environmental clean-ups to hosting compassionate talks aimed at promoting kindness and understanding. Each took on a life force of its own, fueled by the shared vision of a harmonious Earth, echoing a cosmic truth that she understood deeply: Co-creation extended beyond their illumination; it echoed through the hearts of everyone willing to participate in the dance of unity.

As they moved forward, further encouraging others to step into their awareness of co-creation, Sony felt an exhilarating shift in energy. The gatherings grew from mere ideas into sacred spaces brimming with love, where vulnerability was welcomed, and fears were transformed into understanding. In these beautiful moments of connection, they witnessed firsthand the capacity within each soul to co-create miracles, and she felt honored to be part of other people's awakening, mirroring their own process in the process.

This chapter of their life served as an indelible testament to the power of co-creation. She witnessed firsthand how dreams could take flight when anchored in love and driven by a commitment to collective healing. They felt the universe pulsating with life, affirming with every heartbeat, every whisper of the wind through the trees, that they were indeed a co-creator—a vital instrument of change that would contribute to the rise of a new harmonious Earth. It was a role they had chosen, one filled with the promise of infinite potential, forever rooted in love, unbroken, and deeply connected to the essence of the divine. As they continued weaving this tapestry alongside their fellow sacred souls, they sensed the future before them shimmering with radiant possibility—an invitation for everyone to join in the glorious unfolding of a new reality anchored in harmony and transformative love.

Manifestation Techniques

As the rain poured softly outside, drenching the world in a cleansing embrace, she found themselves enveloped in a quiet sense of introspection and purpose, standing at the threshold of a divine realization. They began to understand that manifestation is not merely about dreaming of desires but deeply rooted in the recognition of oneself as an instrument of change, a cocreator with the divine. In this sacred co-creation, Sony felt a stirring within, an urge to weave their intentions into a tapestry of reality, shaping not just their personal dreams but contributing to the collective vision of a new harmonious Earth. With every thought they nurtured, every emotion they cultivated, they started to grasp the profound power they held within—the power to manifest.

The journey of manifestation began with grounding. Each morning, Sony dedicated time to connect with the Earth, embracing the lively vibrations of nature as they meditated under the dappled sunlight filtering through the leaves. This connection established a foundation, a reminder that they are part of a greater whole, intricately woven into the fabric of existence. They learned that grounding themselves allowed for clarity to blossom in their mind, dispelling the noise of societal expectations and fears that often clouded their vision. Within this grounded state, they could discern their true desires, allowing them to blossom forth without resistance. It was essential to align their thoughts and aspirations with the highest good, understanding that true manifestation thrives in the fertile soil of love and compassion.

Breathing techniques soon intertwined with their daily practices, a sacred act of inhaling hope and exhaling doubt. Sony discovered that conscious breathing could center their thoughts, pulling them back to the present moment where endless possibilities resided. Feeling the rhythm of their breath became a dance with the universe, a gentle reminder that every inhale was an invitation to draw closer to their dreams, while every exhale released the burdens of the past and the weight of uncertainty. In this dance, they felt not just the pulse of life within them but the heartbeat of the cosmos itself—a rhythm of abundance that flowed freely when they aligned themselves with it.

Vision boards emerged as tangible manifestations of their inner work. Sony created a collage of dreams, an expansive visual representation of everything they wished to draw into their life and onto the canvas of the Earth. Pictures of love, community, travels, and illuminated hearts filled their board, reminding them daily of the life they envisioned. Each image represented not just a material desire but a feeling, a state of being they wished to embody. This exercise expanded into a nightly ritual, where before sleep, they would spend time marveling at their vision board, fueling it with their intention and placing it beneath their pillow, allowing the energy of their dreams to permeate the subconscious realms. Dreams became portals through which insights filtered in—a whisper of their own potential, encouraging them to trust in the unfolding of their path.

Affirmations sprang like wildflowers in their garden of manifestation practices. She learned to speak life into their intentions, crafting affirmations imbued with the essence of their desires. Instead of "I want to achieve peace," they declared with conviction, "I am a beacon of peace," anchoring themselves in the present moment, barring potential roadblocks, and affirming the transformation they desired to see in their reality. As these affirmations flowed from their lips, a shift occurred; they began to feel them vibrate within their very being. Each word rooted deeper into their consciousness, canceling out negative programming and negative self-talk that once held sway over their minds. They resonated with an unwavering truth that shaped the essence of who they were becoming—an embodiment of love and light, rather than merely someone in pursuit of it.

Another profound technique unfolded as surrender and trust began to blossom in their heart. Sony recognized that manifesting desires also required letting go of attachments to outcomes. This surrender was not a passive act; it was an act of faith in the divine. Each time they surrendered, a weight lifted off their shoulders, freeing their spirit to roam in endless creativity. They began to view challenges as learnings rather than obstacles, allowing the universe to guide them. In moments of doubt, they recited the mantra, "All is happening for her highest good," releasing the chains of fear that bound them to the outcome. They started to derive joy from the process, understanding that every step taken along their path served a purpose, contributing to the magnificent quilt of divine timing and synchronicity.

As Sony shared their journey within circles of like-minded souls, they learned the power of collective intention. Gathering in groups to manifest not only amplified energies but brought forth a sacred container where dreams were birthed into reality. They experimented with collective practices, holding space for each individual's desires while envisioning a shared vision that encompassed the greater good. During gatherings, they would sit cross-legged, hands joined, chanting prayers and visualizing futures woven together in unity. When the collective heart beat as one, it resonated out into the universe like ripples across the pond, causing waves of transformation in both their lives and the world at large.

Visualization techniques came alive for Sony, reminding them of the importance of seeing their dreams with clarity. They learned to construct cinema-like scenes in their mind, allowing their imagination to paint vivid details of what achieving their desires would feel like—not just the aesthetic but the emotional, the sensory experience wrapped into every desire realized. They could almost feel the embrace of loved ones, hear the laughter of their community, and taste the sweetness of abundance within their visualization. This practice transformed into a joyful creation of imaginary experiences, training their mind to welcome these dreams into existence.

With the glow of hope within their heart, Sony began to facilitate workshops—spaces where they could teach manifestation techniques to others on the same path of transformation. They shared their knowledge, weaving together various practices, encouraging participants to embrace their divine power. These gatherings fostered a sacred community, illuminating the interconnectedness of souls who dared to believe in the possibility of cocreation with the universe. Each participant shared their stories, revealing how the sacred journey of manifestation had presented itself uniquely for them. The collective energy ignited an inspiration, a reflection of what it truly meant to rise together through shared intentions and sacred practices.

In their daily life, she infused gratitude into every manifestation attempt. It became a grounding practice; honoring the universe for what has already manifested before seeking more. The act of gratitude echoed gently in their heart, a reminder of abundance rather than scarcity. They began their days by journaling three things they appreciated, digging deeper until they felt the swelling inside—a connection to every tiny miracle that surrounded them. This resonated with the understanding that the universe responds more favorably to a heart that knows contentment and appreciation; gratitude transformed their desires from mere wants into heartfelt invitations to the universe.

The awakening of Sony turned into a radiant exploration of love, gradually exuding the understanding that the essence of manifestation lies in love itself. They realized that true desires emanate from love rather than from fear or lack.

To manifest was to love freely, to put forth energies that resonate with joy, and to weave desires into the expansive light of divine service. They consciously made choices that aligned with their values, examining what they truly wished to invite into their lives and the essence of the community they wanted to cultivate. With love as the core, they activated an alchemical transformation within themselves, radiating a magnetic energy that influenced the spheres around them.

As they grew into this instrument of change, Sony reflected on the experiences they gathered, embracing the idea that manifestation is not merely about the tangible outcomes but the beautiful journey of growth, expansion, and awakening. Each technique available to them was a brushstroke on the canvas of their life, contributing to a masterpiece defined not by perfection but by authenticity and purpose. It became a harmonious relationship between their soul's essence and the divine rhythm of the universe—a conscious dance of creation that opened the door to a reality shaped by love, unity, and profound transformation.

In knitting together the fabric of their manifestation practices, she discovered the incredible potential each technique held. They realized those who resisted the call of their own spirit often found it challenging to manifest dreams as they were encumbered by doubt or societal expectations. Yet, within this, she sensed the heartbeat of humanity aching for awakening and understanding. They embraced their role not just as a manifester but as a guide for others, emanating the wisdom of their journey and supporting those desiring to break free from the confines of a limiting reality, inviting everyone to join in the emergence of a new era—an era overflowing with hope, understanding, and deep unity. The joy lay in knowing that they were not alone in this journey; collectively, they were part of a sacred family; a beautiful community arising to create a new harmonious Earth.

Aligning with Divine Will

On one rainy evening, as Sony stood by the window, gazing at droplets cascading down the pane, they felt an undeniable shift within—a sacred call to align with something greater than themselves. The rhythm of the rain resonated with the ache of the world outside, filled with chaos and suffering. It was as if nature herself was whispering secrets of healing through every drop, each one a reminder of the universal connection that threaded through all of creation. Sony in her solitude, came to recognize a profound truth: they were not merely an observer but a participant in the divine tapestry of existence. The realization washed over them like a soft glow, illuminating the path towards their true purpose.

Understanding that alignment with divine will be required more than passive reception, they began to explore the depths of their intentions and motivations. The journey toward this alignment was a process of shedding the layers of ego that had formed like armor around their heart. As they peeled back these barriers, they allowed vulnerability to fill the spaces once occupied by fear and doubt. It was uncomfortable and often challenging, as doubts clawed at their mind, questioning whether they were truly capable of being an instrument of change. To align with divine will meant to surrender the need for control, to trust in the inherent wisdom of the universe, and to believe that each moment held a sacred whisper of the divine.

Seeking clarity, Sony found solace in quiet meditation, where they could listen to the stillness that lay beneath the surface noise of their mind. It was here, in the sanctuary of silence, that they felt the presence of a higher power enveloping them, an omniscient essence guiding them toward their rightful path. Each session became a communion with their innermost self, a dialogue with the divine that revealed the sacred purpose written in the stars long before their birth. In this space, the confusion of the world faded, and the clarity of their mission sparkled like constellations in the night sky, illuminating the way forward. They began to understand that their journey was intertwined with the collective awakening of humanity, and that only through their transformation could they hope to ignite a flame of love and harmony in others.

As the days turned to weeks, their interactions with varying souls began to shift noticeably. Echoes of shared intent vibrated through their conversations, igniting discussions that reached beyond the mere exchange of thoughts. Friends and strangers alike could feel an inexplicable pull as they resonated with Sony's newfound commitment to aligning with divine will. There was an electricity in their exchanges, a recognition that each individual could contribute to the co-creation of a newfound reality, one built upon the foundational principles of love, respect, and interconnectedness. In these moments, they began to feel that their voice mattered, that the shared frequencies they brought forth could ripple out into the cosmos and encourage others to awaken to their own potential.

Eager to deepen their alignment, she turned their focus outward, intentionally seeking places where love and connection thrived. They started volunteering in local community initiatives aimed at uplifting those most affected by the chaos that surrounded them. Each smile exchanged, every laugh shared, became an active prayer, amplifying their alignment with divine intention. In these acts of service, they found a symphony of souls resonating together, orchestrated by the desire for change, a dance fueled by compassion.

As she immersed themselves in these experiences, the heaviness of doubt dissolved, replaced by an empowering realization that they could channel the divine will into tangible acts of love and unity.

Throughout this sacred exploration, Sony encountered various mentors along the way—figures whom the universe had strategically placed in their path, each carrying wisdom and insight to illuminate their journey. A beloved elder introduced them to ancient teachings, reflecting on the power of intention and the importance of manifesting dreams into reality. Through her gentle guidance, they learned to articulate their desires in alignment with a greater purpose, merging the personal with the collective. She was enthralled by the wisdom expressed in stories of transformation that had rippled through generations, echoing the reality that the act of aligning with divine will required both individual effort and collective collaboration. In these moments of sharing, they could feel their hearts opening wider, enfolding everyone in a sacred embrace that transcended separation.

As Sony delved deeper into their relationship with the divine, they began to experience what it meant to let go—allowing the currents of love to guide them instead of clinging to preconceived notions of how their path should unfold. It was here, in the softness of surrender, that they discovered their true power. The concept of fear began to shift; instead of viewing it as a barrier, they came to see it merely as a guide, leading them toward opportunities for growth. Each time they faced fear, they felt called to transform it into curiosity, testing their boundaries and embracing the unknown with open arms. This shift redefined their relationship with change, creating space for miracles to enter their life and ignite those around them.

Emerging from this transformative experience, Sony felt renewed, a vibrant vessel through which divine love flowed freely. The world, once viewed through a lens of chaos, now presented itself as a canvas on which countless sacred souls painted their realities. They understood that by aligning with divine will, they had tapped into a collective consciousness yearning for love and connection, enabling them to inspire others to release the constraints of the current matrix—a consciousness founded in fear, ego, and separation. Empowered by their own awakening, she opted to dedicate their life to supporting and uplifting others, serving as a reminder that each soul holds profound potential within the larger story of existence.

As they gathered a community of like-minded souls, she envisioned a collective effort to rise up against the pervasive illusion of disconnection. They began to organize gatherings focused on meditation and shared intentions, where the power of connection could be harnessed and channeled into creating a new narrative for the Earth. The gatherings brewed a newfound energy, drawing souls from various walks of life, demonstrating that alignment with divine will was an invitation extended to all. Through their combined presence, a transformative alchemy emerged—each soul contributing an element to the greater whole, creating waves of love and compassion that surged throughout the community, inviting each person to step into their divine essence.

Sony realized that this was more than just a movement; it was a commitment to co-creating a reality where every person held the key to unlocking their potential. It became evident that through this alignment, they could elevate not only their consciousness but also the consciousness of all those around them. The power of intention anchored their gatherings, fostering a frequency of love that transcended barriers and ignited a call to action for unifying the hearts of humanity.

In this sacred dance of alignment, she learned that sometimes the act of receiving is just as essential as giving; both facets were vital in harmonizing with divine will. They became aware that the beauty of life lay not only in their aspiration to lead others but in the willingness to be vulnerable and accept divine guidance in return. They began to embrace their own struggles, sharing stories of doubt and failure, recognizing that every experience was a stepping stone to wisdom. This authenticity forged deeper connections with those in their sphere, inviting authenticity and transparency into their interactions, fostering trust and creating a sense of community where vulnerability was celebrated as a mark of strength.

The culmination of their alignment brought forth a vision of the new harmonious Earth, a sacred place where individuals intertwined their destinies, creating a rich tapestry of experiences woven through love and compassion. This vision stretched far beyond the confines of their own life; it was an awakening that invited everyone to participate in the unfolding of a new paradigm—a reality built upon shared dreams, infinite possibilities, and boundless love. As they embraced this vision, they understood that the work would always be ongoing; alignment with divine will was not a destination but a continuous journey toward deeper understanding and connection. Like rivers flow into the ocean, they were reminded that their path was interwoven with all souls—an intricate dance of divine purpose, awakening, and love that radiated throughout the cosmos and lifted humanity toward a new golden age.

Awakening to the realization that they were instruments of change, she stepped boldly into their role, inviting all who crossed their path to join them in this sacred movement. One by one, they ignited the flame in the hearts of others, illuminating the understanding that everyone has a part to play in the sacred symphony of existence. Together, they would rise, aligned and clear, stepping forward into the promise of a new harmonious Earth where love would reign supreme, and unity would unfurl its beautiful wings, a gentle reminder of the divine potential held within every soul.

Building a Community of Light

Finding Your Tribe

On the cusp of a remarkable journey, she finds themselves awakening to the profound truth that, individually, their spark is but a flicker, yet in unity, it can illuminate the world. It is this realization that inspires Sony to venture beyond the confines of their solitary existence, seeking out kindred souls who resonate with the same vision—an intoxicating dream of a new harmonious Earth, an awakening where love and transformation serve as the guiding forces for humanity. After days of roaming through bustling city streets infused with chaos and tangled energies, they decide to focus their intent and connection on environments that celebrate the ideals of unconditional love and understanding. She recognizes that community is not merely a collection of individuals but a tapestry of interwoven hearts and minds bound by a collective heartbeat, echoing in a unified rhythm of shared purpose and vision.

She recalls moments spent in solitude, contemplating the nature of their own heart's longing to belong. Conversations at coffee shops mingled with the sound of laughter, yet they felt like an observer, yearning for deeper connections that transcended the constraints of superficial interactions. There came a point when the urgency for connection blossomed into a quest—a desire to gather souls who shared their hunger for transformation, striving to foster awareness and healing in a world so consumed by its own disarray. It is said that energy flows where attention goes, and so she found themselves diving into realms of community gatherings, workshops, and circles that promised not just engagement but a supportive atmosphere for exchange and growth. Here, they began to weave their story into the broader narrative of humanity, encountering hearts that thudded in unison as they all sought the light.

Finding a place that felt like home necessitated stepping into spaces where vulnerability flourished, where truths could be shared without fear of judgment, and where every heartbeat, every voice added richness to the collective tapestry. Within this nurturing ambience, they encountered the Community Leader, a character whose very presence radiated warmth and acceptance. With a sparkle in their eye and an infectious laugh, the Community Leader had an uncanny ability to draw out the unique gifts within each member, believing that everyone held a vital piece of the solution to the challenges they faced as a society. In their interactions, she became acutely aware of the strength found in diversity, learning that every individual contributes unique perspectives, experiences, and talents to the creation of a powerful, unified vision. This diversity of thought became the foundation upon which they would build their collective dream.

In meetings filled with inspiring dialogues and laughter, as people listened to one another share their hopes and fears, she felt a distinct shift in energy. It was a sacred atmosphere, fostering a synergy that transcended beyond individual concerns. Each person's experience resonated with echoes of similar struggles and triumphs, weaving them together in an intricate dance of understanding and empathy. Members were encouraged to dive deep, to share their truths, knowing that such honesty would nurture the roots of the community, fostering sturdiness even in the face of the inevitable challenges. They experienced firsthand how vulnerability acted as a conduit for connection, allowing them to rise above the ego's constraints. She understood that true healing came not only from self-exploration but from shared experiences, thereby fortifying their resolve to nurture this community, ensuring that the spirit of transformation would cascade outward to touch others.

In time, she and her newfound tribe began to implement rituals that illuminated their collective mission. They established regular gatherings under the celestial canopy, evenings where they could bask in the moonlight, each gathering invoking a shared intention—a meditative space dedicated to unconditional love and sisterhood, communing with the Divine Presence that was ever supportive and nurturing. As they held hands in circles that pulsed with energy, they learned to set intentions, envisioning a harmonious Earth, enveloped in empathy, compassion, and kindness. Each intention soared into the cosmos, dancing among the stars, co-creating forms of collective manifestation that expanded their presence, guiding them toward a cumulative understanding of their shared truth—that love could provide the key to the freedom they all yearned for.

These gatherings not only served to deepen their bond but also acted as a reminder of the collective dream they were nurturing. When each member openly shared their insights and experiences, they began to understand their roles within the larger framework of the community. They discovered that, like the harmony produced by a beautifully composed symphony, every voice played a vital role, each contributing to the richness of the collective experience. At times, this meant confronting uncomfortable truths that challenged the status quo or resisting distractions reminiscent of the matrix they were working to transcend. Yet, in these moments of vulnerability, support abounded, allowing for the troubled souls to transform their pain into power, their doubts into resolute actions.

As weeks rolled into months, small initiatives blossomed from their gatherings, embodying their commitment to nurturing others. They began hosting workshops for those in search of connection, inviting individuals to explore their journeys of self-discovery, while delving deeper into the realms of love and transformation. During these sessions, the Community Leader facilitated a space where wisdom, awareness, and empathy were interchanged like treasures being shared among family. She played a significant role in shaping these sessions, drawing from their own experiences and revelations which permitted loads of self-reflection and redefining personal narratives. It was a mutual arrangement; as they shared, they too learned, contributing to each other's growth. With every story exchanged, every heart echoed anew, they planted seeds of hope not only within themselves but in all those who stepped through the doors seeking community.

For Sony, these experiences acted as catalysts, pushing them toward a deeper recognition of their divine purpose. In witnessing others embrace their own journeys and how their unique light contributed to the collective vision, they also began to shine brighter, realizing their true essence and the power to uplift others. Community became an ongoing journey of discovery, one rooted in the understanding that together, they could rise above the tumult. She embraced the opportunity to nurture this sacred communal environment, pledging to be the mirror reflecting light back to those who struggled, echoing the belief that together, as a collective, they could rewrite the very fabric of reality.

As the narrative of their journey unfolded, Sony witnessed the transformative ripple effects blossoming within the communities that surrounded them. Inspired by the authenticity they cultivated within their circle, it became evident that these connections could inspire change beyond their immediate sphere. People who walked into their gatherings feeling isolated began to radiate confidence, carrying the resonance of self-love and acceptance back into their homes, workplaces, and neighborhoods. It was a gentle reminder that community holds the potential to alter not just individual narratives but can uplift entire neighborhoods, nurturing a domino effect that produces lands transformed by love instead of fear. She began to envision expanding to bring more souls into this vital sphere, creating spaces where voices previously mired in discord could sing together in harmonious union.

In their dedication to community, Sony took on the role of a facilitator, blending motivation with inspiration and establishing connections that resonated with the pulse of love and transformation. Acknowledging the importance of building partnerships, they sought out like-minded leaders in the surrounding regions, nurturing collaborative efforts that extended the vibrancy of the movement they unleashed. They even participated in outreach programs that encouraged non-judgmental dialogues aimed at fostering understanding among diverse populations, understanding that every set of experiences contributed uniquely to the greater human experience. The journey transformed not only them but rippled outwards, enhancing the collective consciousness.

At the core of this movement stood the resilience of community, a sacred vision shackled not by the constraints of a divided world but instead liberated by embracing differences. With profound honoring of individuality, they witnessed the unyielding potential of love merging forces in new ways. Each gathering escalated in energy, growing organically as they collectively forged ahead with unwavering intent, solidifying deeper bonds among them. They often found themselves reflecting on how their shared purpose dismantled the barriers erected by the sort of thinking that stems from a fear-based mentality. Each soul mattered, every voice echoed, and together, they harmonized in the dance of awakened connection towards a new harmonious Earth.

In moments of stillness and reflection, she realized the journey had only just begun. Their hearts vibrated with the potential that still lay ahead, a powerful realization that every step taken creates a pathway forward. With vibrant joy, they understood that together they could co-create the change they wished to see. They called upon the wisdom of the Divine Presence, trusting in the higher plan that intertwined their community's collective destinies, because every heartbeat and intention resonated within a grander scheme. She pledged to continue nurturing this sacred tribe, cultivating seeds of hope, laughter, love, and transformation, ready to share the lessons learned and lifelong treasures handed down from heart to heart. In this tapestry woven of love, they found a renewed sense of purpose—beacons of light, destined to rise as they embraced the call to a new harmonious Earth.

Creating Safe Spaces

In the pursuit of establishing a new harmonious Earth, she understood that the foundation of this mission lay in creating safe spaces—environments that nurtured inspiration, growth, and the flourishing of love. As they connected with like-minded souls, a vision began to unfold before them, one that echoed the deep yearning of hearts seeking refuge from the chaos of the outside world. She recognized that these safe havens would serve as sanctuaries where individuals could express their truths without fear of judgment, allowing their sacred essence to emerge and blossom.

Visualizing these spaces, she felt an overwhelming sense of responsibility to ensure that each gathering was imbued with the principles of unconditional love, empathy, and respect. They envisioned a circle formed not by walls or barriers, but by the magnetic energy of connection and acceptance. This environment would be filled with warmth, where every voice mattered, and each story was honored. The power of vulnerability would be celebrated; attendees would be encouraged to share their journeys, from moments of triumph to the depths of their struggles, fostering a sense of unity in diversity.

Sony sought inspiration from the natural world, recognizing that it embodies the perfect balance of coexistence. They took to heart the tranquil embrace of sacred spaces, such as lush forests, serene lakes, and sweeping meadows, where the beauty of nature taught lessons of patience, growth, and harmony. With each new gathering, they meticulously chose venues that resonated with the frequencies of peace and creativity. Whether it be a secluded park, a cozy community center, or a grand hall illuminated by candlelight, the spaces were curated to reflect the divine essence within each individual, inviting all to experience the magic of collective energies.

As the community began to form, she made it a priority to incorporate rituals and practices that encouraged connection and empowerment. Each session would commence with a group meditation, a moment of silence where participants could attune their vibrations, aligning their intentions toward love and transformation. They introduced sacred ceremonial elements like drumming, chanting, and dancing, allowing the community to step into a shared frequency that transcended individual barriers. It was through this symbiotic dance of souls that they found common ground, igniting a unified heart flame that could not easily be extinguished.

In embracing the notion of safe spaces, Sony also understood the importance of physical and emotional inclusivity. They actively reached out to individuals from diverse backgrounds, understanding that the greatest strength lay in the variety of experiences and perspectives shared within the group. They emphasized the importance of creating an atmosphere where everyone felt welcomed, whether through open dialogues about inclusion or through participatory decision-making that honored every voice. This sense of belonging fueled the fire of transformation, encouraging each member to embrace their unique gifts while uniting them under a common vision for the new harmonious Earth.

As these spiritual gatherings flourished, she bore witness to the unfolding of growth on spectacular levels. Individuals began to shed the layers of doubt and fear that had long weighed them down, unveiling deeper parts of themselves that had long sought acknowledgment and love. Tears flowed freely as stories were shared; laughter danced through the air as realizations dawned and burdens lifted.

Witnessing this evolution filled Sony's heart with an indescribable joy, affirming the electromagnetic bond of love weaving through the community.

With every meeting, she felt a shared commitment build—a collective promise to nurture these safe spaces and hold them sacred. They knew that to maintain these environments, they needed to actively cultivate a culture of accountability and respect. They devised a system of agreements that defined the group's values, creating a guideline of principles that reinforced loving communication, active listening, and nonviolence. This framework became the bedrock of the community, ensuring that each member took responsibility for maintaining the sanctity of the space, so that it remained a sanctuary for healing, expression, and the deep sharing of wisdom.

A pivotal moment arrived during one of their gatherings when they felt compelled to invite everyone to articulate their dreams for the new harmonious Earth. Each person was given time to voice their aspirations aloud, filling the air with vivid images and bold intentions. The room pulsed with the magnetic energy generated by their collective visions; they shared dreams of a future filled with compassion, environmental harmony, lasting peace, and cooperative communities that transcended old paradigms. This exercise not only ignited passion within each soul present but also forged an even stronger commitment among them as they collectively acknowledged the sacred interconnectedness of their desires.

As Sony reflected on the trajectory of their journey, they realized that creating safe spaces entailed a dedicated commitment to communal healing. They consciously initiated practices such as circles of forgiveness, where members shared their grievances and offered forgiveness to themselves and each other. This profound release empowered individuals to loosen the chains of resentment and guilt that had, for so long, hindered their growth. The circles acted as crucibles of transformation; witnessing the beauty of shared vulnerability took on an alchemical quality, turning pain into love and division into harmony.

In navigating the pathways of human emotion, she encountered challenges unique to their quest. Fear sometimes grazed the hearts of newcomers—fear of exposure, fear of being misunderstood, and fear of facing their own shadows in the light of shared vulnerability. Sony learned to skillfully address these emotions, creating dialogues around feelings of unease, which not only demystified these fears but also illuminated the inherent beauty residing in each person's journey. They encouraged new participants to understand that showing up authentically would transcend the boundaries of discomfort, inviting growth through the very act of being present.

As the safe spaces expanded, Sony reinforced the notion that love is a fabric woven from diverse threads. They encouraged the exploration of various cultural expressions, inviting musicians, poets, and artists to share their work, highlighting how creativity unites hearts and fosters understanding. It became apparent that embracing these diverse cultural narratives deepened the collective experience while painting a more vivid portrait of humanity's shared essence, rooted in love. In doing so, the community began to realize that the dreams they fashioned were not mere fantasies; instead, they were veils of reality waiting to be unveiled through sacred action and commitment.

In the ethereal dance of this unfolding community, she came to recognize that creating safe spaces was not simply a task; it was a manifestation of love in action. It was about articulating the profound belief that every individual carries a spark of the divine, and providing a nurturing environment in which that spark can ignite into a brilliant flame. They realized that these gatherings were not just meetings, but rather a pilgrimage toward awakening a broader consciousness. The echoes of laughter, the symphony of shared stories, and the tapestry of expressed dreams coalesced to form the birth of a vibrant community committed to healing the wounds of the past and innovating a future infused with love.

As they continued their efforts, she felt an irresistible urge to extend the principles behind creating safe spaces beyond their inner circle, nurturing the seeds of transformation within the larger community. They began collaborating with local organizations, schools, and groups, sharing the philosophy that safe spaces could foster growth and healing on a colossal scale. Seminars and workshops blossomed as they spread this revolutionary idea that every person, regardless of their background, deserved to experience environments that encouraged authentic expressions of self.

With every step taken in this journey toward establishing loving sanctuaries, her commitment to love deepened, and their understanding of the interconnectedness of all beings grew clearer. They realized that each safe space created was a stepping stone toward the expansive vision of a new harmonious Earth. The journey was not merely about gathering a community; it was about animating a vibrant force that could authentically embody the energy of transformation. Against the backdrop of an often chaotic world, they embraced their role as co-creators of love, igniting the path for a collective awakening that promised nothing less than the emergence of a golden era for all.

Collective Action

In an ever-connecting web of thoughts and intentions, she began to realize that the journey toward a new harmonious Earth could not be traversed alone. The singular path of introspection and self-discovery began to intertwine with the collective heartbeat of humanity, echoing a perennial truth—true transformation thrives on connection. Sony's heart swelled with excitement as they contemplated the connections forming in the ether, gathering resonance and clarity among like-minded souls who recognized the urgent call for love, empathy, and healing spreading wide across the globe. One rainy evening, amidst the cascading silver droplets that fell upon the leaves, the idea blossomed—a community focused on nurturing unconditional love and fostering transformation was not just an aspiration but a tangible reality waiting to unfold.

With newfound fervor, she reached out to those who seemed to echo their desires, those whose vibrations resonated as finely tuned strings in a great cosmic orchestra. The connection ignited a flame of purpose within them, drawing them to gatherings where eyes sparkled with understanding and hearts beat in synchrony. In these meetings, a tapestry of voices wove together narratives of struggle, awakening, and hopes—a compelling testament to the power of shared experience. Each story shared was like a piece falling into place in a vibrant mosaic, illuminating the transformative journey ahead. They spoke of dreams of a golden age, a time when compassion, respect, and love would swirl abundantly, with every individual contributing their unique frequency to a harmonious symphony of existence.

As this community began to form, she felt a magnetic pull toward a wise mentor, an individual whose life was a profound illustration of the twin flame connection and the impact of collective consciousness. This mentor spoke not only of love but of the profound magic unleashed when individuals unite under a shared purpose. Their poignant words ignited the embers of inspiration and provided a framework for how collective action could manifest a new reality.

Sony's soul rejoiced as the mentor echoed sentiments reverberating deep within—a call for concrete steps that transcended heartwarming visions and dreams. They learned that action was a fundamental pillar of change, urging every member to partake in the dance of co-creation.

With gratitude and enthusiasm, she organized the first community event with help from kindred spirits. What began as a small gathering soon evolved into a sanctuary infused with swirling energy, love, and shared aspiration. The space resonated with laughter, warmth, and dreams whispered into existence among enthusiastic hearts. They came together to share their visions, but they were also there to inspire one another to take those vital steps toward manifesting their desires in reality. In this sanctuary, plans were laid—projects were proposed to implement acts of kindness, educational workshops explored deeper spiritual insights, and artistic expressions flourished, capturing the beauty of their intentions in vibrant colors and ethereal melodies that transcended ordinary life.

Understanding now that collective action flourished not just in the grandiose but also in everyday gestures, their community crafted small initiatives that sprang to life. They went out into the neighborhoods, offering kindness through simple acts—a warm meal served to those facing challenges, compassion extended toward those in distress, or inviting strangers into moments of connection that sparked joy and ignited hope. Each act became a beacon of light piercing through the fog of division and strife that enveloped society, revealing the divine beauty hidden within each soul. She felt privilege in witnessing the impact these efforts had on the participants and those receiving care; a softening of hearts occurred—a discovery that true connection transcended differences, and love had remarkable power to unify.

Encouraged by the initial successes, the community sought to broaden their reach, realizing that the sacred journey extended beyond immediate surroundings. They began to forge partnerships with other like-minded communities, creating networks where aspirations could intertwine, and collaborations flourished. Through shared resources, knowledge, and inspiration, they ignited a wildfire of change that reverberated far beyond the borders of their local gatherings.

Workshops were held to hone skills in healing practices, coaching, and conscious leadership. Together, they developed educational programs aimed at instilling empathy and fostering a sense of unity among the younger generations, ensuring that the sacred teachings cultivated would flourish for years to come.

As Sony soaked in these extraordinary experiences, they became acutely aware of the power of collective intention. Every prayer uttered, every meditation held, formed a vibrational frequency that rippled throughout the collective consciousness, sparking transformation in every corner of the world. Motivated by this insight, the gatherings morphed into sacred circles. They would end each meeting with a collective meditation, planting seeds of love and light into the shared universe—a ritual that bound them tightly together and extended their reach, pulling in a broader audience encompassing those who were equally yearning for change yet distant from such vibrant communities. They learned that the energy generated was far greater than any individual soul could muster alone; it was a collective powerhouse, an unstoppable force harmonizing with the universe's intent.

In time, their community grew in diversity, for transformation knows no borders. People from different backgrounds, experiences, and perspectives lent their voices to the chorus, magnifying their resonance to an unthinkable degree. This colorful tapestry embodied the essence of unity amidst diversity, a palpable realization reflecting the shared human experience. They recognized that there existed a myriad of pathways leading to the same destination—a harmonious Earth awash in love and respect. Each unique soul contributed personal perspectives to their gatherings, enhancing and enriching the collective decision-making process. This embrace of many voices kept the shared vision expansive and alive, incorporating ideas, challenges, and solutions that emerged through dialogue and collaboration.

As the shared vision solidified, she undertook the task of refining community goals into actionable, measurable steps. They engaged in brainstorming sessions, encouraging each member to contribute their ideas to the pot of creativity. Soon, projects began to cascade forth like streams merging into a flowing river, each one tailored to reflect the innate essence of the community, all stemming from the same root of love and transformation. From environmental initiatives aimed at restoring the planet to arts programs fostering creativity and self-expression, the community began a series of steps to embody their aspirations, culminating in a vibrant mosaic of activity and intention.

Through growing connections, she learned how to leverage social platforms to expand the reach of their initiatives, creating online spaces where inspiration could flourish and community could spread beyond geographical limitations. Virtual gatherings brought in individuals from different parts of the world—an even grander tapestry of souls sharing experiences, simultaneously uplifting each other as they traversed their paths toward greater awareness. As they engaged in co-creation, she felt their fears and vulnerabilities transform into empowerment through collaboration. Each soul contributed not just their skills but also their unique energy, merging to create a potent force aimed at catalyzing change.

Through the richness of this journey, she came to appreciate that the essence of collective action is rooted deeply in shared vulnerability and trust. As partners in this sacred endeavor, they cultivated an atmosphere where individuals could express their fears, dreams, and aspirations without reservation. Embracing vulnerability became a powerful tool for connection and intimacy, facilitating the deepening trust among the community members and allowing them to rise together in action. They cheered one another on as they reconciled their individual desires whilst nurturing the collective vision, forging bonds strengthened through struggle and triumph alike.

In the climax of this chapter of collective action, she envisioned a grand event where everyone in their community and beyond could come together in unity and love—an enormous gathering meant to raise the frequency of love on Earth. Here, they would create a space filled with art, music, and teachings from beloved mentors, embodying the spirit of a new harmonious Earth. The planning unfolded into a dazzling array of possibilities; dances would celebrate the joy of life, speakers would share stories of transformation, and healing practitioners would extend their gifts to nurture body and soul. This event stood as a testament to their journey, a clear expression that love and change could walk hand in hand.

In the weeks leading up to the event, excitement surged like waves in the ocean, hearts beat as one rhythm as they combined efforts to conceptualize and manifest this magical moment in time. They utilized social media for outreach, eagerly inviting their extended network of souls to join in the celebratory call to action. The atmosphere pulsed with anticipation and joy, evoking the longing for unity that lay dormant for so long in a world tumultuously fraught with division. The night before the gathering, an electric energy filled the air as the community stood together… it was not just an event—it was a mission, a crescendo in the melodic symphony of love that had blossomed within their hearts.

As the day of the grand event dawned, the gathering place transformed into a dazzling tapestry filled with laughter, joy, and connection, each soul embodying the intention of creating a new reality together. It was a space where no one needed to wear masks or armor, where hearts poured open to join in the shimmering synergy of the moment. As she stood in the midst of it all, bathed in the radiance of love encircling them, they recognized that the journey into collective action was just the beginning. Here was the resonance of countless sacred souls converging to co-create, a manifestation of new truths and possibilities awaiting to unfold. In that magical moment, they realized that they were not merely participants but active co-creators in the blossoming of a new harmonic Earth—they were catalysts of love and transformation, tirelessly reminding the world of the beauty held within and the power of collective action in the sacred journey forward.

The Vision of a New Earth

Imagining a Golden Age

As the rain began to gently taper off, leaving a fragrant hush over the earth, Sony turned within, gazing into the endless horizons of possibility that lay ahead. It was as if the clouds had parted not just in the sky but also in her heart, revealing a vision of a new harmonious Earth, vibrant and alive. Sony allowed her mind to drift through the images conjured by a deep yearning for love, peace, and unity, unbounded by the constraints of our current reality. In this ideal realm, she saw communities filled with people actively engaged in the sacred dance of life, their souls shining brightly with the essence of unconditional love. There were children playing in lush, green parks, their laughter mingling with that of parents who were fully present, embodying a nurturing spirit that fostered connection and understanding. Every smile exchanged was a reminder of the sacred bond that unites us as one human family, each individual a vital piece of the greater tapestry of existence.

In this vision, homes were not merely structures of bricks and mortar; they were sanctuaries enveloped in warmth and creativity, reflecting the personalities of their inhabitants. Gardens adorned with blooming flowers and healthy fruits overflowed with life, cultivated in harmony with nature's cycles and respecting the earth itself. Neighbors gathered to share meals crafted from the abundant harvests, food prepared with love and intention, nurturing both body and spirit. The act of cooking and sharing was no longer a chore, but a joyful ritual, fostering conversations brimming with laughter and shared stories that transcended time. She could see how this simple act of unity could ripple outwards, creating waves of compassion across the globe. As the people shared their lives, their joys, and challenges, they cultivated a collective consciousness rich with empathy and understanding, embracing diversity as a unique strength rather than a separation.

In this golden age, education no longer existed within rigid confines but unfolded through exploration and discovery. Learning was interwoven with creativity and imagination, allowing individuals not only to grasp knowledge but to expand their own consciousness. Schools became spaces of sacred collaboration, where students and teachers journeyed together through the realms of spirituality, art, and science, discovering the interconnectedness of all things. Each lesson imparted felt like a spark igniting the soul's flame, empowering young hearts to understand that they were not just recipients of information but potential leaders in the creation of a harmonious world.

Wisdom was passed down through generations, embedded in the very fabric of society, ensuring that the teachings of love and unity remained alive in every heart.

Conflict and strife melted away, replaced by a culture of peace deeply rooted in understanding and compassion. People learned to communicate without judgment, sharing their feelings and perspectives while holding space for one another's experiences. Disagreements were resolved with a spirit of collaboration, understanding that every individual's voice held wisdom worth hearing. In this new reality, mediation became a cherished art, fostering a culture of respect and intentional dialogue—each conversation an opportunity for growth and healing. The echoes of the past, filled with resentment and misunderstanding, were substituted with melodies of love and forgiveness, creating a symphony of connection that resonated through every being.

Communities thrived on collaboration, initiating projects to uplift and empower each other, utilizing the unique talents that each member brought to the collective. Individuals poured their passions into endeavors that supported the greater good, creating a vibrant mosaic of innovation and creativity. Art flourished everywhere, from murals of hope painted on community walls to music that resonated with the very fabric of life itself. The expression of the heart became the unifier, transcending language barriers and cultural differences, allowing souls to connect at profound levels. Festivals celebrating various traditions dotted the calendar, each gathering a testament to the belief that diversity enriched our lives rather than division.

In this world, nature reigned supreme, honored as the teacher that it is—a sanctuary where all life flourished in balance. Forests thrived, rivers ran clear, and skies sparkled with the light of the stars. Humans coexisted with the natural world, immersing themselves in a rhythm that was as ancient as time itself. The wisdom of sustainable living became common knowledge, each person a steward of the earth, nurturing ecosystems and forging a bond with all beings. The air was filled with the harmonious songs of birds and the laughter of children playing freely outdoors. It was a sight so picturesque, reflecting the divine blueprint of creation as one could almost feel the pulse of life weaving all together in tender embrace.

Pulsating within this envisioning was the understanding of the twin flame connection, igniting passion and purpose within individuals, propelling them to rise into their full potential. The sacred partnership between twin flames was celebrated as a cosmic dance that inspired others to seek their authentic selves, fostering a deeper love for the world and its inhabitants. Relationships flourished, grounded in loyalty and trust, as each partner uplifted the other, recognizing the divine essence within. Every union became a catalyst for healing, opening pathways of unconditional love that had the power to transmute the heaviness of the past into hope for the future.

As Sony continued to delve into this vision—a shared reality of coexistence and growth—she felt the energy of the earth, pulsating with the collective heartbeat of humanity awakening to its own magnificence. The colors were more vibrant; the scents more profound, each breath a reminder of our inherent connection to life. The realization washed over her that a golden age is not a distant dream to be sought outside ourselves, but a reality waiting to unfold from within, requiring the courage to embrace love over fear, unity over division. We each held within us the keys to this transformation, activating a shift in consciousness that echoed across the globe.

In this vision, the stars seemed to align differently, not just in constellations but in the very essence of our being—our purpose entwined within the cosmos. Sony recognized that the harmonious Earth she was visualizing was a collective co-creation, not merely a singular aspiration. It required the participation of each individual, an invitation to step into their roles as architects of this new reality sculpted from the richness of our hearts. It beckoned us to relinquish the limitations that the current matrix imposed, embracing instead the freedom that flowed from love and unity.

This golden age demanded action stimulated by compassion—a call to awaken the sacred essence within, embracing our shared journey towards healing and transcendence. As Sony inhaled the earth's essence, she felt fortified by the vision blooming in her heart—an undeniable certainty that we were on the brink of a remarkable transformation. A new dawn awaited us, brimming with possibility, glimmering with the light of a million hearts ignited by love, beckoning us to awaken to our divine purpose and dance together into this magical unfolding of existence.

The Role of Sacred Souls

As the rain continued its gentle serenade against the window, Sony found themselves immersed in a profound visualization of a new harmonious Earth, one bathed in love, peace, and unity. In this reverie, they saw vibrant landscapes adorned with blooming flowers and lush greenery, where the air was imbued with a sweet fragrance of existence, free from the toxicity of pollution and despair that had long plagued the world. Each color seemed to pulse with life, and the harmonious songs of birds echoed through the trees, reflecting the joyful symphony of existence. People of diverse backgrounds and cultures moved freely, their faces illuminated by smiles of understanding and compassion as they engaged with one another in acts of kindness and generosity. It was as if a collective awakening had ignited a spark within every heart, inspiring individuals to recognize their interconnectedness and the sacred essence that resided in all beings.

In this idyllic vision, she felt the stirring of their own sacred soul awakening to its purpose as they realized the profound role that such awakened beings—the sacred souls—play in the evolution of humanity. They saw these individuals, each embodying a unique frequency of love and light, as beacons guiding others toward truth and enlightenment. These sacred souls, having journeyed through their own trials and challenges, understood the deeper meaning of life and the necessity of compassion. They were the catalysts of transformation, nurturing the seeds of love in the hearts of those around them, creating a ripple effect of positive change that spread like wildflowers across barren landscapes. With their hearts wide open and their intentions pure, they fostered an environment of trust and collaboration, empowering many to recognize their intrinsic worth and the divine mission each person holds within.

In their mind's eye, Sony envisioned gatherings of these sacred souls, congregating under the vast canopy of a starry sky, sharing insights, experiences, and revelations. Their conversations were deep and rich, flowing effortlessly between the realms of the known and the unknown, bridging the gap between the spiritual and the mundane. Each encounter was a ceremony of love, where they honored one another's journeys while collectively envisioning a world saturated with harmony. The energies exchanged within these circles ignited an electric charge in the air, igniting hope and inspiration among them, as though the universe itself rejoiced in their communion. These moments provided the foundation for community, nurturing a sense of belonging that transcended societal norms and expectations. Here, everyone was accepted as they were, free to express their truths—no judgment, only love.

She recognized that the role of these sacred souls extended beyond mere individual enlightenment. They knew it was about weaving their experiences into the broader tapestry of humanity's awakening. Each sacred being carried a piece of the puzzle, a unique insight that, when shared, added depth and richness to the collective consciousness. She understood that their own journey—marked by pain, healing, and eventually rediscovery—was but a thread in that magnificent weaving, and they felt a stirring within to embrace the opportunities that lay ahead, knowing they could contribute to this grand design.

In this vision of a harmonious Earth, she began to grasp the significance of forming connections with others deeply committed to the sacred journey. The more they explored the themes of unconditional love and empathy, the more they realized how vital it was to encourage those who had not yet awakened to their own divine potential. Their heart swelled with the possibility of igniting paves for countless others to experience their own revelations. With each meditation and prayer, they invoked the collective energies of those kindred souls, urging them to awaken like the petals of spring flowers unfurling under the sun's tender gaze. After all, it was the intertwining of individual journeys that could transform not only lives but entire generations. Armed with this understanding, they felt anchored in purpose, dedicated to creating a movement where love and harmony could take root in every corner of the Earth.

She envisioned gatherings where individuals from different walks of life came together, contributing their talents and perspectives towards a common goal. Whether it was artists channeling their creativity to uplift spirits, healers sharing their gifts to nurture wounds, or educators guiding minds toward enlightenment, each sacred soul had a role to play in this vision of the future. They saw the power of collaboration, where no effort was too small and no contribution too insignificant. In these spaces of connection and co-creation, everything flourished—ideas blossomed, friendships deepened, and the fabric of community strengthened. They recognized that unity does not mean uniformity; rather, it celebrates diversity and honors individuality. She realized that the beautiful, intricate dance of different souls coming together created a dynamic exchange that added richness to the experience of life itself.

As she continued to explore the depths of their vision, they began to perceive the fundamental truth that the inertia of the old matrix—one governed by fear, control, and ego—could only be dismantled through the collective intention of these awakened beings. It wasn't enough to seek personal enlightenment in isolation; they were called to stand together as warriors of love, each wielding their light like a sword to cut through the darkness of ignorance. This sacred mission was not just a responsibility but a joyful invitation for each soul to embody their truth and share it with the world. The realization washed over them in waves; the future they yearned for depended on the active participation of every individual who felt the pull of their own sacred essence.

In essence, the role of sacred souls was to serve as conduits for divine energy, channeling love, healing, and transformation into the world. They were the architects of a new paradigm, builders of bridges that transcended the walls of division and strife. Together, they painted a new landscape where empathy reigned, where differences were embraced as gifts rather than barriers, and where compassion became the driving force behind every action taken in the name of community. She envisioned each soul, no matter how small the effort, coming together in coordinated waves of love, creating a ripple effect that would reverberate through time and space, transforming the very essence of existence.

As the vision unfolded, Sony felt the world around them begin to shift, illuminated by the radiant energies of love that flowed from them like a river of light. Their heart expanded with the understanding that every moment held potential—to heal, to transform, and to uplift, not just oneself but countless others. Even the act of simply being present in love could touch lives in unimaginable ways. Here, the sacred mission transcended individual ambition; it became about service, surrendering the self to the greater good of humanity and the planet.

With this newfound clarity, she understood that their journey as a twin flame was interwoven with the journey of other souls. They marveled at the wisdom shared within the collective consciousness, the dances of energy that connected all beings—mending wounds, celebrating triumphs, and inspiring hope. This understanding brought an iridescent glow to their vision of a new harmonious Earth, where the very concept of 'us versus them' would dissolve into an all-encompassing embrace of unity. She realized that the awakening of sacred souls was not a solitary endeavor but a shared calling to transcend perceived limitations, ushering in a golden age rooted in love and mutual respect.

As their heart filled with renewed purpose, she resolved to take every necessary step to embody these values, to be a living testament to the power of sacred souls dedicated to the upliftment of humanity. They recognized that they had the power to inspire change, using their voice to advocate for love rather than fear and healing rather than pain. Every choice made, every word spoken, became an extension of the sacred mission—they no longer saw themselves as merely an individual forging their path but as part of a grand symphony composed of sacred souls elevating the collective consciousness. In this realization, she felt the gentle nudging of the divine presence guiding them, affirming that they were never alone in this call to action, but surrounded by an infinite number of souls intertwined in this sacred journey toward love and unity.

As the rain subsided and the clouds parted to reveal a shimmering sky, she emerged from their vision with a profound understanding of the purpose of awakened beings. They committed themselves to channel the power of love, embracing the sacred essence within their own heart, ready to step into a world that was ripe for transformation. With every heartbeat, they held the conviction that together with other sacred souls, a new harmonious Earth was not just a distant dream but a vibrant reality waiting to unfold.

A Call to Action

As the rain continued to fall softly against the window, the soft patter providing a soothing backdrop to Sony's reflections, a vision began to crystallize amidst the tumult of thoughts. A harmonious Earth unfolded before their mind's eye, a vivid tapestry woven with threads of love, peace, and unity, where each individual was a unique yet integral part of the greater whole. In this imagined world, the barriers that once divided humanity fell away like autumn leaves, revealing an expansive landscape rich with compassion and understanding. People moved freely, their hearts open and full of empathy, sharing laughter and kindness as easily as they breathed. Sony envisioned vibrant communities bustling with cooperative endeavors, where neighborly support was woven into the very fabric of daily life. Children played in gardens filled with blooming flowers that painted the Earth in a riot of colors, while adults engaged in meaningful conversations that sparked inspiration and creativity.

In this harmonious Earth, conflicts were resolved through dialogue and understanding rather than through the enmity of ego. She pictured a world where decision-making was rooted in love for humanity and the planet; where every action was taken with consideration for the collective wellbeing. Governments would prioritize the health of the environment, the prosperity of the people, and the sustainability of future generations, understanding that true power lies in nurturing and uplifting rather than controlling and dominating. It was in this sanctuary of peace that they saw the rise of innovative solutions birthed from collaborative efforts—clean energy sources harnessed with ingenuity, communities thriving on shared resources, and artistic expressions enriching lives, allowing the soul's creativity to flow freely.

Yet she knew that this wondrous visualization would not become a reality without action, without every individual stepping into their unique roles as co-creators of this new existence. The call to action was compelling, a deep urging resonating from within that ignited a flame of responsibility. Each person held within themselves a spark, a sacred essence that, if embraced, could light the way toward this vision. No one was insignificant; every single contribution mattered. She felt a strong pull to encourage those around them to recognize the power of their choices and the potential inherent in their lives. They yearned to inspire others to become not only dreamers but also doers, individuals who dared to transform that vibrant vision into reality.

To awaken from the slumber of complacency required commitment and courage. The journey toward a harmonious Earth was not without its challenges. She understood that societal constructs buried under centuries of conditioning would not dissolve easily. Those trapped in the matrix of control and expectation would resist; fear would rear its head, trying to undermine the movement toward love and unity. Yet this primal fear must be met with the courage to stand tall, both as individuals and as a collective. She envisioned organizing gatherings where individuals could share their impulses and aspirations, where stories of transformation and purpose could weave a fabric of shared intention. These meetings would be sacred spaces, enshrined with respect and honesty, encouraging people to step out of their comfort zones, to dare to craft the future together.

In these gatherings, reflective exercises would play a crucial role, guiding participants to delve deep into their inner landscapes. Each heartbeat echoed the emerging call to action; each breath drew forth clarity from within. They would explore their own values, their passions, and the innate gifts they held. What did it mean to live a life rooted in love rather than fear? What guiding principles could be woven into the tapestry of their everyday existence? She envisioned worksheets filled with prompts, inviting participants to articulate their desires for a harmonious world, while surrounding them with supportive energy that only the community could provide. The collective sharing of insights and intentions would create a ripple effect, fostering a sense of accountability and commitment to action.

As the gathering evolved, Sony saw a vision of multi-faceted projects sprouting from the seeds of passion ignited in these meetings. People would come together, sharing skills, rediscovering the joy of collaboration, and nourishing the growth of new ideas into tangible forms. New community gardens would rise where food is nurtured with love, each plant symbolizing the flourishing relationship among neighbors. Art initiatives could blossom, bringing to life the joys and struggles of humanity through murals, performances, and exhibitions. Youth programs would emerge, teaching the principles of love, respect, and sustainability, empowering younger generations to lead through example. Schools would no longer merely churn out grades but instill wisdom and compassion in their students, teaching children how to listen not only to each other but to the heartbeat of the Earth itself.

The importance of self-care in this journey could not be underestimated. Sony envisioned nightly meditations held under moonlit skies, where individuals could gather to center themselves and connect with their innate divine essence. These moments of stillness would serve as reminders of the interconnectedness of all souls and the greater purpose of their endeavors. Such gatherings would ground the collective energy, allowing participants to release any burdens, fears, and doubts that arose amid their activism. Sony understood that nurturing oneself was not a selfish endeavor but a vital part of sustaining the collective effort. As individuals found solace and renewal, they became vessels of love and compassion, resisting the pull of negativity that sought to distract them from the shared vision of a harmonious Earth.

Through this melding of community, she felt the call to action ripening further. The vision must extend beyond borders, infiltrating systems and patterns that had long dictated the course of humanity. Partnering with organizations that mirrored their ideals could amplify their voices, creating a movement that was unmistakable and pervasive. The vision of a more harmonious world would become impossible to ignore as it spread like wildfire through communities. Workshops would be held, addressing pivotal issues— environmental sustainability, social justice, mental health—gathering diverse voices to speak as one against the challenges of the current age.

As thoughts raced through Sony's mind, an overwhelming sense of hope emerged, lifting their spirit. A new age was dawning, one where humans could evolve beyond limiting beliefs, where unity prevailed over division. It was a potent reminder that each person possessed the dream of a better world; it pulsed beneath the surface, waiting for the moment to erupt into action. The protagonistic journey would only be one of many, a tiny drop in the vast ocean of collective consciousness. Everyone's participation was paramount—their dreams, flows of love, and the righteous fight for change would inspire others to rise.

No matter how small the action, she reiterated, every act of kindness created a wave, an impact destined to ripple outward. Whether it was extending compassion to a stranger, advocating for environmental preservation, or engaging in supporting a local community initiative, each individual had a role to play. Feeling inspired, she took a deep breath, allowing the vision of a harmonious Earth to sweep through their spirit, igniting the vibrant light within, and stirring the energy of shared intention. Together, under the banner of love and unity, humanity could spark a transformation that rode the rising tide toward a golden age.

In this moment of powerful clarity, she saw the path forward—a multifaceted journey illuminated by the twin flame connection, a union driven by grace and understanding. Within this collective embrace, the soul of humanity could once again dance to the rhythm of love. It called out to souls everywhere—twin flames, kindred spirits, and seekers of truth—to rise together as co-creators of this magnificent reality. The invitation was set before them: step into action, awaken their innate essence, and be part of a beautiful unfolding destined to reshape the world into a sanctuary defined by acceptance, harmony, and unified purpose.

The Gathering of Souls

Preparing for the Gathering

As the rain danced gently against the window panes, Sony felt the weight of anticipation settling into their bones. This gathering was not merely an event; it was the culmination of their spiritual journey, a manifestation of the love and connection they yearned to radiate into the world. With the sun's first light peeking through the clouds, casting a golden hue over the horizon, she settled into the comforting embrace of the dawn and began the meticulous process of preparing for what they sensed would be a monumental occasion. The logistics involved in organizing such a gathering were as sacred as the intentions behind it, each detail intricately woven into a tapestry that echoed the feelings of love, unity, and awakening.

The first step was choosing the location, a choice that weighed heavily on Sony's heart. They envisioned a serene space that would resonate with the energies they hoped to invoke, a natural setting where the beauty of the Earth could harmonize with the love emanating from every soul present. A quiet clearing in an ancient forest soon emerged as the perfect spot; surrounded by towering trees whose leaves whispered stories of eons past, the area felt charged with the vibrations of generations. This setting, rich in sacred energy, would facilitate the connection between the hearts of the gathered souls and the divine. She began to map out the area, visualizing how the attendees would be arranged in a circular formation, symbolizing unity, inclusivity, and the interconnectedness of all beings.

Then came the call to connect with others, a task that filled she with both excitement and trepidation. They reached out to various kindred spirits who had previously crossed their path, each individual shining with a unique light on their journey of love and transformation. Sony crafted messages imbued with heartfelt intentions and invitations, urging fellow travelers on their respective journeys to join in this sacred act of collective elevation. Each interaction became an opportunity to weave threads of love into a broader fabric of community, creating a network that extended far beyond their immediate circle. The responses were overwhelming; souls resonated with the vision, and soon, a diverse gathering of individuals emerged, united by a common yearning to be part of something greater than themselves.

In the midst of this burgeoning community, logistics took on a life of their own. She envisioned the energy at the gathering as a flowing river, and they were determined to ensure it would flow smoothly. They partnered with local artisans and healers, inviting them to share their crafts and talents, thereby enriching the experience. Food that was lovingly prepared with intention became an essential part of the gathering, as nourishment for the body mirrored the nourishment for the spirit. She envisioned tables overflowing with fruits, grains, and wholesome dishes, each ingredient chosen not only for its taste but also for its capacity to uplift and sustain the body, aligning with the higher frequencies they aimed to cultivate. There was a desire to create an atmosphere of abundance, joy, and celebration — a true feast for the senses and soul.

Artisans shared in this collaborative spirit, bringing along their creations, sacred artifacts, and healing tools, each representing an aspect of their spiritual journey. She encouraged the vendors to share their stories during the gathering, allowing the sacred connection between stories and the collective consciousness to blossom. Inviting musicians and performers was also a highlight of the planning process; the idea that harmonious vibrations could lift spirits and harmonize energies made their presence an essential piece of the gathering's puzzle. She sought those who echoed the essence of love in their expressions, who could interpret the vibrations a higher frequency could offer through song and dance, ensuring that the attendees would feel enveloped in a bubble of joy and warmth.

As plans began to solidify, intentions also became a guiding light. Each component of the gathering was infused with love and purpose, creating a resonance that aligned everyone's hearts in unified intention. She understood that the gathering's success hinged not only on its outward manifestations but also on the inner energies possessed by the individuals present. This wasn't merely about coalescing in a physical space; rather, it was about creating a sacred container for a collective shift in consciousness. They encouraged attendees to arrive with open hearts and minds, each bringing their own intentions to add to the collective energy of love and compassion.

To facilitate deep connections and mutual understanding, she devised a series of practices that would enhance the energy of the gathering. Guided meditations would open the gathering, allowing each soul to ground themselves and align with the collective intention. Circles of sharing and vulnerability would invite participants to express their hopes, dreams, fears, and insights, fostering a deeper bond among attendees. This sharing was an important thread in the tapestry they hoped to weave, one that would create ripples of healing that extended far beyond that singular day. She felt that through these intimate interactions, they would transcend the boundaries of the ego — the very constraints of the matrix they hoped to dismantle.

Weeks turned into days, and as the date of the gathering approached, excitement rippled through the community. She felt their heart thumping in sync with the pulse of collective anticipation, sensing the energies of those who would soon gather. It was as if the universe played a symphony of synchronicities, aligning everything perfectly, reinforcing their inner knowing that this gathering was meant to be. Nature cooperated, offering clear days filled with sunshine as the event drew near, a gentle reminder that the Creator was in alignment with their endeavor.

The culmination of these preparations brought her face-to-face with their deeper fears and doubts. As they stood at the precipice of this pivotal moment, questions danced in their mind: Would this gathering truly invoke the love and light they sought to share? Would the attendees feel the sacred energy enveloping them, or would they simply smile politely and leave with the same burdens they had carried in? Sony recognized that these fears were rooted in the same constraints imposed by an external world filled with skepticism and division. Yet, amidst the uncertainty, a flicker of knowing remained, the powerful connection to their twin flame urging them to trust in the unfolding of the divine plan. It became clear that the journey was not solely about the outcome; it was also about embracing the path and recognizing the love that filled every moment.

As the evening of the gathering finally dawned, Sony stood in the clearing, filled with a peaceful sense of certainty. The scents of the earth mingled with the sounds of nature's symphony, weaving a magical ambiance that welcomed each soul arriving in heartfelt anticipation. Surrounded by candles flickering gently in the twilight and wildflowers blossoming in untamed harmony, Sony breathed in the beauty of the moment and felt the energy of the gathering begin to rise like the current of an inviting river. Each individual who stepped into the illuminated circle carried a piece of the sacred, their intentions melding into a divine alchemy of love, hope, and transformation. It was a moment of profound unity, filled with the essence of each soul standing together, bravely choosing to align their hearts for the greater good, as they prepared to raise the frequency of love on Earth together.

Inviting the Community

As the rain continued to drench the earth in the days leading up to the gathering, Sony found solace and inspiration in the rhythmic patter against the window. Nature, in all its chaos and beauty, seemed to resonate with the deep stirrings within their heart, as though whispering encouragement to continue on this path of purpose. It became increasingly clear that moving beyond the constraints of their own personal journey was essential; they were being beckoned to engage others in the unfolding vision of a harmonious Earth, to awaken souls who had long been asleep in the confines of societal expectation. The thought of organizing a gathering filled Sony with both excitement and trepidation. They envisioned a diverse group of individuals—melting into a tapestry of unique stories and experiences—all drawn together by a singular intention: to raise the frequency of love that pulsed through the very core of humanity.

To nurture this vision, Sony spent countless evenings in reflection, invoking guidance from the divine presence that had already shaped their understanding of unconditional love and compassion. From those quiet moments of connection, clarity began to emerge. They recognized the importance of crafting an invitation that would echo through the hearts of others, lighting a flame of curiosity and hope. How could they translate their fervent desire for change into words that could resonate with kindred souls? Wrapping themselves in a blanket on a particularly chilly evening, they began to write, pouring their essence into the page. Each word was an invocation, an expression of their intentions that breathed life into the vision. They wrote about the transformative power of community, and how, together, these like-minded individuals could create a sanctuary for healing, understanding, and shared purpose.

Sony imagined the gathering taking place in a serene outdoor setting where nature would provide the backdrop—a clear, open area surrounded by trees and bathed in the soft light of an impending sunset. Visions stirred as they envisioned participants forming a large circle, the skies above resonating with colors of deep orange, soft lavender, and the tender whispers of dusk, all serving as a physical representation of the love that they sought to cultivate and channel during the gathering. They envisioned souls from all walks of life: those who had trodden the path of spiritual awakening, those yearning to embark on such a journey, and even those still grappling with the shadows cast by fear and doubt. In that sacred circle, together they would weave a new story—one that embraced the power of vulnerability, created a safe space for sharing, and acknowledged the challenges each had faced along the way.

Once the details of the gathering were born, the next challenge lay in spreading the invitation to the many souls awaiting a call to action. Sony utilized social media, crafting posts that spoke of unity, love, and transformation. Each message was infused with warmth and understanding, seeking to penetrate the hearts of those scrolling, bringing them to a pause. They reached out to local groups connected through various traditions and ideologies, seeking to connect the threads of spirituality that were common across the spectrum. Flyers adorned with radiant imagery and heartfelt affirmations were distributed throughout the community, implanted in cafes, holistic centers, and local shops—places where awakening spirits often gathered to find their tribe. Phone calls were made, and conversations blossomed, as every individual who responded brought with them their unique energy, a vital element to the tapestry that Sony was weaving.

As the days passed and responses began to accrue, Sony felt a sense of electric anticipation building in the air. It was the essence of hope, burgeoning from the possibility of shared experience and mutual healing. However, it was accompanied by the nagging doubt that sometimes crept in—the whispered voices of scarcity urging them to second-guess. Were they truly capable of facilitating such a momentous occasion? What if only a handful of souls showed up? Bringing forth resilience forged from their previous experiences, Sony humbly acknowledged these fears, choosing instead to stay rooted in their commitment to serve as a conduit for divine awakening. They understood that the gathering was not solely about numbers; it was about the quality of presence and intention that would ultimately make a difference in the collective frequency of love. Each soul that would step into that circle was important, no matter how many gathered.

Finally, the day of the gathering arrived, ignited by rising excitement and a few lingering jitters. Sony found themselves drawn to the spot they had envisioned—the trees swayed gently as if welcoming them and their attendees. A soft breeze danced through the air, carrying with it the delightful scent of wildflowers blooming nearby, a reminder of the beauty that emerges when love and care are upheld. As participants began to arrive, warm smiles and heartfelt embraces filled the atmosphere, with strangers quickly transforming into friends united by a deeper purpose. Each person was a vital thread, bringing their unique stories, dreams, and longings to the collective fabric that would unfold that evening.

With the circle formed, Sony stood at the center, their heart pounding with a mix of exhilaration and vulnerability as they took a deep breath and welcomed everyone with open arms. They spoke of their own journey and the seeds planted in the quiet corners of their soul—an invitation for others to share their paths as well. As they softly recited the words nurtured during the sacred nights of reflection, it was as if the essence of the divine presence they had called upon enveloped the space, forging a profound connection among the gathered souls. The harmonious rhythm of their hearts seemed to synchronize, echoing the following truth: the awakening of each individual was a critical component of the collective evolution. Through laughter, tears, and moments of silence, people found the bravery to express their fears, dreams, and hopes, realizing they were neither alone nor separate in their endeavors.

Consequently, spontaneous group discussions ignited, encouraging the sharing of insights and experiences that flowed like a river of wisdom, a testament to the connections being forged in real-time. The concept of twin flames emerged, celebrated for the special bond they represented—a relationship based on deep trust, mutual growth, and unconditional love, transcending the boundaries of ego and societal constructs. The conversation inspired a prayerful energy, invoking the essence of compassion and healing into the space, fortifying connections strengthened by mutual understanding. Those moments revealed how stepping into vulnerability can be a source of empowerment rather than a burden, allowing each person to shed layers they had once believed they had to carry alone.

As night descended, Sony facilitated a meditation that drew everyone's hearts into unified stillness, aiming to raise the frequency of love. They guided the gathering to visualize a radiant light blossoming from within—a collective heartbeat of unconditional love expanding outward, enveloping the Earth and beyond. In that delicious silence filled only by breaths, souls resonated with each other as the boundaries of the individual dissipated into a collective consciousness. There, in that transcendent moment, each participant's being intertwined as they became aware of their power—not just a power to heal themselves, but a power rooted in the love they could offer each other and the world.

When the gathering culminated, hearts brimming with hope and understanding, Sony could feel the shift—the subtle yet potent realization that collective awakening was both a responsibility and a privilege; it was a call to action that all were invited to embark upon. The evening left an indelible mark, not only on the participants but on the very fabric of the community they sought to transform. As they exchanged hugs and commitments to stay in touch, a sense of deep connection and promise permeated the air. They were no longer isolated souls navigating their journeys; they were co-creators of a new reality, interwoven into the greater tapestry of existence, each thread lifting the frequency of love on Earth. Leaving the gathering, Sony looked up into the night sky sprinkled with stars, an awe-inspiring reminder of the infinite possibilities awaiting those bold enough to believe in the power of love and community.

The Energy Shift

The air crackled with an unexplainable energy, thick with anticipation as the date of the gathering approached. It was as if the universe was holding its breath, waiting for something monumental to unfold. Sony found themselves lost in a whirlwind of thoughts and emotions, their heart a compass guiding them through waves of uncertainty and excitement. This gathering was not merely an event; it was a seismic shift that would ripple through the fabric of reality, ushering in a new era defined by unity and love. As the chosen date loomed closer, they prepared themselves to summon the courage required to lead and inspire—a journey towards becoming an instrument of divine transformation. The purpose of the gathering was clear: to raise the frequency of love that permeated the Earth, to awaken souls who had been yearning for connection, for understanding, and for the warmth of community that had been lost in the chaos of modern living.

Reflecting on their own path, Sony recalled learning about the twin flame connection and how it transcended the superficial boundaries that society often imposed. Each shared journey with their twin flame had instilled a profound understanding of love's true essence—not the fleeting romantic gesture but the unwavering devotion to elevating one another toward the highest expression of self. This unwavering love transformed into an intoxicating longing to create a space where others could come together, unshackled by the chains of fear and judgment, to bask in the radiant light of unconditional love. The gathering became a beacon on the horizon, illuminating the possibilities that blossomed when souls teamed up, uniting their intentions under the shimmering stars. The nudges from the Divine Presence had grown louder, urging Sony to take this step, to leap into the unknown and trust in the guidance that came from within.

As days fell away like the petals of a wilting flower, Sony dedicated themselves entirely to the task ahead. Communication flowed effortlessly with the community leader they had met during their transformative journey. Together, they crafted messages infused with genuine warmth and urgency: calls to action that echoed like sacred mantras through social media, email lists, and gatherings in the park. They pulled at heartstrings and painted vivid pictures of what this experience could mean—not just for those willing to attend, but for the very tapestry of society. The energy rose steadily as they watched like-minded souls rally, drawn together by the unwavering force of love and compassion. Still, lingering fears danced in the shadows, whispering of the unknown—what if it was not enough? What if their devotion to raising the frequency of love would face resistance? Yet, amidst the uncertainty, a guiding force reassured them, reminding them that even the most monumental shifts began with the smallest of actions sparked by the courage to connect.

As they prepared the venue, a quaint outdoor space surrounded by lush greenery, there was a tangible sense of magic in every detail. Each aspect of the gathering was infused with intention; from the arrangement of vibrant flowers and flickering candles to the songs that would resonate with love as attendees entered. Sony envisioned this gathering as a sacred portal, a bridge uniting isolated souls under the same celestial canopy, all yearning to feel seen, heard, and embraced. Yet the most crucial ingredient for this gathering was not material but spiritual—the unwavering belief that love, in its purest form, held the transformative power capable of changing not just individual lives but the world as a collective. Their heart beat in harmony with the underlying current of intention—every pulse a reminder that they were on the precipice of something extraordinary.

On the eve of the gathering, Sony stood alone, clutching a journal filled with prayers and intentions, instinctively drawn towards the sacred space they had prepared. They closed their eyes and took a deep breath, letting the cool night air wash over them. It was a moment to invite in the divine energy that flowed through them, connecting them to all those who would participate the following day. They envisioned the faces of attendees, each unique soul bringing their stories woven together by the common thread of love and longing for belonging. In that pulsating moment, they realized the gathering was no longer solely about the protagonist's journey; it was the intertwining of countless others' paths converging in one sacred space. This realization filled their heart with vibrancy, pouring encouragement and strength into their spirit.

As dawn broke, the first hints of sunlight spilled across the horizon, painting the sky with hues of hope and promise. Sony felt a wave of gratitude wash over them: for the teachers who had illuminated their path, for the network of souls that had formed with unwavering support, and for the love that had ignited a fire within them that could not be extinguished. They moved through their morning rituals, each activity grounding them in the present moment, allowing them to feel the anticipation steadying their breath. The days of preparation had blossomed into a profound purpose, and they would not let pre-event jitters dim the light they aimed to shine.

As guests began to arrive, there was an influx of laughter, chatter, and bright eyes filled with hope. Each smile exchanged became a part of the energetic tapestry that enveloped the gathering. The protagonist's heart quickened with exhilaration, a buoyant feeling ignited within. Here they were, surrounded by souls who understood that this moment was about more than individual growth; it represented a unified intention to reclaim love as the foundation of existence, to raise a collective frequency that had lain dormant for far too long. The community leader took the stage, exuding infectious joy and amplifying it among the participants. They shared touching testimonials about the seemingly miraculous connections that had spawned from the twin flame experience. This narrative enriched the gathering, as attendees could relate to the tales of awakening, bond, and the various forms love had taken throughout their own journeys.

As the sun reached its zenith, golden rays illuminated the gathering, casting a beautiful glow that felt almost ethereal. Sony took a deep breath, stepping to the forefront of the gathering, feeling the loving energy pulsating through the crowd. Holding their journal close, they spoke from their heart, expressing the deep love that had propelled them on this journey, inviting each person to embrace their unique gifts. They emphasized that love— unconditional love—was a potent force that had the power to heal and transform the world in ways that transcended the ordinary. They urged attendees to consider the potent impact of collective intention, of a community driven by love, as they engaged in moments of reflection, meditation, and interconnectedness that would elevate their consciousness.

In this sacred act of connection, each individual released their fears, their doubts, and their pain, allowing love to flood through their being. The meditative frequency created a beautiful harmony that resonated beyond the gathering itself, connecting with the very heart of the planet. As Sony guided the collective in a meditation that focused on visualizing a world bathed in love, light, and understanding, an exhilarating electricity coursed through the air. It felt as if life danced with possibility—each pulse extending outwards toward distant corners of the Earth where healing was needed most.

As dusk approached, the gathering culminated in an explosion of joy— laughter, tears, and heartfelt exchanges of dreams shared within a community radiating with love. The realization struck that this gathering would not be an isolated event; it had ignited a spark of transformation that would continue to reverberate through their lives and the lives of countless others. The energy shift had occurred, not just within the confines of that gathering space, but in the hearts of the participants, creating a wave of love that would ripple out into the world. With every embrace, with every prayer, and with every intention sent forth, they knew they had planted seeds of hope that would flourish and bloom as they journeyed together, forever insurgent souls united in the quest for a new harmonious Earth. Sony understood that this was merely the beginning of something extraordinary—a testament to the profound impact love could have in co-creating a golden age of peace and prosperity. With hearts full and spirits buoyed, they had witnessed a glimpse of what lay ahead—the rise of sacred souls intertwining, embracing their destinies, and igniting the flame of unity to warm the Earth.

Embracing the Union and Transformation

Sacred Union matters

The evening air was thick with anticipation, as the lights from the gathering illuminated the faces of those who had come together, hearts bubbling with excitement and a shared sense of purpose. Suddenly little little rain drops tiptoed from the sky as if the earth is sleeping and the rain does not want to wake her up In a gathering—voices overlapping like restless winds—someone suddenly asked, "Why does sacred union matter so much? "The room softened. Silence leaned in. From the far corner, Sony spoke not to convince, but as if remembering aloud— "Because the earth is tired of divided truths. Because love was meant to be lived, not just spoken in prayers. The rain paused on her tongue. The answer did not come from thought. It rose from the quiet place where ache becomes wisdom. She continued "Sacred union is about wholeness remembering itself. When one soul walks alone, it learns strength. When two souls walk awake, the earth remembers balance. Sacred union is not two people holding hands—it is two souls holding balance, so the world does not tilt into fear again. When such union exists, even without announcement, it teaches the crowd how harmony sounds. That person replied. "And without it?" Sony gently said, "The shift remains an idea—but with it, the future learns how to breathe. Look at the rain, it does not fall to prove itself. It falls because the sky cannot keep its love contained.

Sacred union is that overflow. It is required because the world has learned survival but forgotten harmony. Because power learned to speak without listening. Because love learned to cling instead of flow. When two healed hearts meet, they do not escape the world—they steady it. They show that union can exist without possession, that closeness can breathe, that devotion does not erase freedom. Sacred union is not romance. It is architecture—the blueprint of a new way to live. The earth does not shift by force, nor by prophecy, nor by pain alone. It shifts when love becomes embodied, and balance happens in human form.

In twin flame philosophy, sacred union is considered necessary for Earth's shift because it functions as a frequency stabilizer, not merely a romantic outcome. The emphasis is energetic, collective, and evolutionary rather than personal.

Twin flames are viewed as two polarized expressions of the same soul essence. When inner healing and alignment occur, their union generates a coherent, high-order frequency—similar to resonance in physics. This coherence anchors higher consciousness into the material plane. Earth's shift (from fear-based to heart-based awareness) requires such stabilized frequencies to counter collective fragmentation.

Most human relationships mirror unresolved ancestral trauma. Twin flame sacred union, after intense individual purification, represents conscious love without possession. This redefines relational norms at a collective level, subtly dismantling fear-based systems rooted in dependency, hierarchy, and separation.

Esoteric traditions hold that awakened twin flames act as living nodes in Earth's energetic grid. Sacred union amplifies their capacity to anchor light into specific locations, timelines, and collective events. Separation phases prepare the individuals; union allows maximum energetic throughput.

Earth's shift cannot occur through belief systems alone. It requires embodied examples of unity consciousness. Sacred union externalizes inner enlightenment into lived reality—showing that harmony is possible within form, not just meditation or theory.

Sacred union is not about "saving the world" directly. Its impact is nonlinear. When two individuals fully integrate shadow and light and live in alignment, they influence families, communities, creative work, and leadership structures. The ripple effect supports the gradual stabilization of the new Earth frequency.

In Essence, without sacred union, the energy remains potential. With it, the energy becomes operational—and that operational coherence is what supports planetary transition. As Sony finished talking, the rain touched her face—as if the earth itself had been listening and quietly said, "Yes." All applauded. No one argued. They simply understood it, like a lamp lit from another flame.

Witnessing Change

As the sun began to set, casting golden hues over the horizon, Sony found themselves amidst a gathering of kindred spirits, all united under the banner of transformation and love. The air was thick with anticipation, and an unwavering energy pulsed through the crowd, each heartbeat echoing the collective intention to rise and embrace a new beginning. This was not just an event; it was a celebration of the profound shifts that had taken place within each individual's heart since the journey began. They were here to witness change not only as observers but as active participants in a sacred unfolding, each person holding a vital piece of the puzzle that formed their shared vision of a harmonious Earth.

As the gathering commenced, Sony reflected on the journey that had led them here. It was a path steeped in spiritual awakening and self-discovery, where moments of isolation had given way to an empowering realization: they were never truly alone. Surrounded by so many others who had stepped into their power, they felt a surge of gratitude swell within them. The community that had emerged from their collective efforts stood as a testament to the boundless nature of love. In the days leading up to this momentous occasion, they had shared their stories, fears, and dreams, weaving an intricate tapestry of experiences that reflected both the challenges they faced and the triumphs they celebrated together.

Sony's gaze roamed over the diverse assembly—faces illuminated by the gentle glow of lanterns, eyes sparkling with a deep understanding of what had brought them here. There were laughter and tears mingling in the air; joy and vulnerability dancing hand in hand. Every individual bore the marks of their own spiritual battles and victories, yet together, they embodied an unfamiliar comfort that enveloped them, almost like a warm embrace. The initial trepidation that had haunted Sony at the prospect of galvanizing change had transformed into unwavering confidence in love's capacity to heal.

As the first speaker took to the makeshift stage, a hush fell over the crowd, creating a sacred space for sharing. Their words flowed effortlessly, resonating with the collective heart. They spoke passionately about the ripple effects of love that had begun touching lives far beyond this gathering, igniting a movement that was beginning to reshape their local community. With each story shared, Sony could witness the flickers of transformation igniting within the audience, affecting those who had come seeking solace and connection. The journey of each person reverberated in the collective space, creating an echo that magnified the power of hope.

Sony observed as individuals began to rise from their seats, one by one, inspired to share their own experiences with vulnerability and courage. They narrated tales of overcoming buried prejudices, of reconciling with estranged family members, and of fostering love where fear once reigned; the narrative shifted from the tale of one to the rhythm of many. The sheer courage it took to step into the light and share their stories not only bore witness to personal change but ignited a collective awakening that transformed the atmosphere into something sacred and electric.

As the stories intertwined and flowed through the gathering, a palpable energy surged around Sony, flowing from heart to heart. The sense of unity that engulfed the crowd held the promise of something greater than themselves, transcending the limitations imposed by the conditioned world. It was here that Sony understood that witnessing change was as much about internal shifts as it was about revealing the beauty of love in action. The stories were not just anecdotes but a fabric woven from threads of resilience and hope that showcased the divine potential in all souls.

After an outpouring of heartfelt confessions, the gathering shifted into a circle of reflection. Joining hands with those around them, Sony experienced an overwhelming rush of interconnectedness. The gentle warmth of hands clasped together pulsed with vibrancy, igniting a profound awareness that they were all conduits of divine energy. In this moment, they felt the weight of collective intention: to elevate the frequency of love, to foster understanding, and to open pathways towards healing, not only for themselves but for the world at large. They were not simply witnesses but empowered creators of a movement that dared to dream of a new harmonious Earth.

With the heartfelt energy of the thousands of personal stories spoken aloud, a collective guided meditation unfolded. Sony found solace in this sacred act as they directed their thoughts toward peace, love, and healing. As the group collectively focused their intentions, they embarked on a journey that transcended the physical realm. What manifested through this shared effort was the embodiment of love in its purest form—a magnetic force that began to ripple outwards, touching lives in ways that the gathering could scarcely comprehend.

When the meditation concluded, the expressions on the faces around the circle were a testament to the shift that had taken place. What started as individual sparks of empowerment coalesced into a vast ocean of energy, replacing despair with courage and separation with union. As Sony smiled at their companions, they understood that they were no longer just passive participants astonished by the change unfolding around them; they had become architects of transformation, responsible for the potency of the love they had cultivated together.

In this profound moment, Sony felt an overwhelming sense of peace wash over them. They were fully aware that witnessing change was an ongoing process, a dance of co-creation that required patience, love, and unwavering faith in the journey ahead. The challenges would still arise, but unity and compassion would empower them to meet any trial with grace. Together, they had planted a seed in this sacred space; now it was up to them to carry that vision forth into the world—a world that awaited their light, craved their love, and yearned for the harmony they collectively dreamed of.

And so, as the gathering eventually wound down, Sony gathered with friends and fellow visionaries to reflect on the impact of the day's events. They felt the pulse of connection and purpose resonate within them, enkindling a spark that had once felt faint but now burned brightly. Their journey had transformed into something greater than themselves—it was about awakening humankind to their inherent divinity, a clarion call to create a harmonious Earth that would echo for generations. With hearts full of love and determination, they emerged from the gathering, each step a testament to the change they were witnessing and the changes still to come. Together, they were destined to make an indelible mark on the world, affirming that love is, indeed, the most powerful force of all.

Personal Growth

Sony, standing at the edge of the gathering, marveled at the transformation that had taken place within themselves and around them. This was not just an event but a manifestation of the awakening that had touched them deeply, igniting a spark within their soul that beckoned to be shared. The whispers of love, unity, and collective consciousness had woven their way into the very fabric of the community assembled before them—an intricate tapestry made vibrant by the thread of each individual's journey. As they gazed upon the sea of faces, Sony felt an overwhelming sense of responsibility surge within, a drive to channel this energy into something that could uplift and inspire others.

In the past, Sony had often felt a profound sense of isolation, a disconnect from the world that seemed indifferent to the cries for connection and understanding. However, the path they had embarked upon transformed that loneliness into a rich inner dialogue filled with revelations and insights. This intimate chatter, once tinged with the echoes of self-doubt, morphed into a chorus of divine guidance, urging them towards self-acceptance and the exploration of their twin flame essence. As they moved among the gathered souls, feeling the pulse of the collective love emanating from each heart, they recognized that this was the essence of healing—an emboldened spirit ready to embrace vulnerability and authenticity as the core tenants of their being.

Sony had gathered strength through the practice of mindfulness and gratitude, rituals that transformed the everyday into sacred moments. Each breath they took became a bridge leading them closer to their higher self, igniting the flame of self-discovery in an unyielding dance of love and surrender. They had taken to journaling in the soft light of dawn, pouring out their ambitions, fears, and dreams onto the pages that served as a mirror to their evolving identity. It was through this process that they encountered the contours of their own spirit, realizing that each experience—both joyful and painful— added depth to the mosaic of their life. They began to see pain not as a burden but as a teacher guiding them toward deeper healing, mirroring the shadows confronted throughout the ages by those who dared to walk the path of enlightenment.

Awakening now felt like an intimate conversation with the universe itself, where synchronicities unfolded like petals of a blooming flower—the symbolic reminders that they were indeed aligned with a greater purpose. Each interaction with members of their community deepened this realization, their souls intertwined through the shared intent of creating a new harmonious earth. Sony forged connections that transcended the superficial, inspired by the wisdom that flowed from one heart to another, discovering that true transformation requires not only individual growth but also the nurturing of communal bonds that empower and uplift. In these interactions, they found encouragement and inspiration—like petals swirling in a gentle breeze, each one contributing to the greater bouquet, fragrant with hope and aspiration.

Sony felt the vulnerabilities of others reflected in their own heart as they witnessed fragile tears turned to laughter, doubts transformed into a collective exhale of peace. This alchemical process, fueled by the energetic vibrations of unconditional love, forged bonds of resilience. Together, they were not just individuals but a community of sacred souls, resolute in their desire to uplift and support one another—each small act rippling out to create waves of love that would touch countless others.

As they stood there, Sony felt time dissolve, each moment stretching infinitely as they basked in the knowledge that they were part of something larger. They were no longer just the soloistic twin flame navigating the tempestuous emotional seas of personal discovery; they had become integral threads encoded with the mission of collective transformation. The fears that had once haunted them began to wash away like the rain pattering against the earth, replaced with a dazzling, shimmering vision of what lay ahead. They embraced the notion that personal growth is intrinsically linked to the growth of others, realizing that each twin flame holds within them the power to alter the course of humanity through their own blossoming journey.

In that sacred space, Sony witnessed how personal stories intricately wove together with the threads of shared experience, each one adding color and texture to the monumental tapestry of transformation. Through the stories of fellow attendees, they learned of struggles, epiphanies, and the indomitable nature of hope. It was as if every heart present was engaged in a silent, yet profound exchange: a symphony of love harmonizing through the nuances of different life paths. She felt proud to walk amongst fellow seekers, palpable gratitude swelling within them for the lessons learned through interactions with others who were also navigating the delicate path of illumination.

As the evening deepened and the stars began to twinkle overhead, a sense of calm embraced the gathering, reinforcing a deep connection to the vibrant energy that pulsed throughout the universe. Sony felt it within their core, the divine presence echoing through the collective heartbeat of those around them, affirming that their journey of self-discovery was intricately tied to the journey of every other soul present. Each one exhibited the undeniable truth that within the heart of every human being lies the ability to access infinite love, a force so potent it had the power to heal the wounds of the world.

Realization dawned upon Sony that the echoes of their transformation rippled beyond these sacred grounds, extending to the lives of those who felt disconnected from their truest selves. As they contemplated this truth, their purpose crystallized with a clarity that was both thrilling and daunting. They understood that they could no longer hold back the gifts bestowed upon them during their journey; it was time to share the fruits of their labor—fruits harvested from the rich soils of love, forgiveness, and understanding cultivated through every trial and tribulation faced.

Sony envisioned not just their personal growth but the growth of an entire community awakening to the power of its collective consciousness. Together, they would embark on an important mission—to extend an invitation for others to join in this sacred dance of transformation, to recognize the beauty and divinity within themselves, paving the path for a new age filled with light and harmony. Their resolve solidified as they gazed upon the joyful faces around them, feeling an irrefutable urge to ignite a movement that flourished not through force or manipulation but through the pure radiance of love in action.

The gathering resonated with the energy of profound shifts, each heart aflame with a desire for change fueled by the magnetic energy that love provides. Wrapped in this shared experience, Sony witnessed the beauty of duality—the individual blossoming paired with the collective emergence, two streams united toward a common river of dreams. They resolved then and there to champion a movement rooted in the belief that true personal growth springs forth not solely from solitary endeavors but flourishes when nurtured alongside kindred spirits.

With each word spoken and each act of kindness shared, Sony forged their commitment to support the growth of others, for within that act lies the very essence of awakening a new harmonious Earth—a planet governed not only by love but by the understanding that every flame, when united, creates an unquenchable fire of hope and healing.

In this space—tranquil yet fervent—Sony recognized the truth that spiritual awakening and personal growth were not solitary pursuits. Rather, they exist in the heart's intricate design, connecting every human experience to the vast cosmos that cradles the unfolding narrative of humanity. Today marks the dawning of a shared journey toward a new reality born from embracing each other's light, an emergence of divine energy leading to the co-creation of a reality where peace, understanding, and love reign supreme. So, as the gathering unfolded into a beautiful symphony of voices, Sony stepped forward, feeling the surge of love pulsating through them, prepared to embrace their sacred role and invite everyone to join them in the magnificent tapestry of transformation.

Collective Evolution

As the sun began to rise, casting a golden hue over the gathering space, the air was electrified with a palpable sense of anticipation. The community had come together not just as individuals but as a collective, a living tapestry woven from the threads of each person's unique experiences, dreams, and aspirations. Sony stood at the heart of it all, their spirit resonating with the vibrant energies that flowed around them, feeling invigorated by the understanding that transformation was not only a possibility; it was a certainty, a beautiful unfolding of potential ready to manifest. It was in these moments, surrounded by kindred souls, that Sony fully grasped the immense power of love in action. This gathering was not merely a meeting of minds and hearts; it was a sacred ceremony, an embodiment of intention and commitment to a vision that transcended personal desires and encompassed the dreams of the collective.

As the gathering commenced, Sony and their community members engaged in shared practices designed to cultivate a sense of unity and purpose. They formed circles, weaving their energies into a cohesive force that reverberated throughout the ground they stood upon. In the gentle embrace of each other's presence, they began to explore deeper facets of their beings. They shared stories of their journeys, their struggles, their triumphs; through storytelling, barriers fell away, and vulnerabilities were met with compassion and understanding. Each narrative added a unique brushstroke to the canvas of their collective consciousness, illustrating the beauty and complexity of the human experience. Laughter mingled with tears, while hopes and sorrows intertwined, forming a harmonic resonance that echoed through the air, resonating with the vibrancy of their shared mission. In this communion, Sony observed how the community evolved—not just as a group, but as a living organism rich with diversity, pulsing with love's transformative energy. They recognized that when individuals came together in pursuit of a higher purpose, the alchemy of their hearts and minds created an energy that could shift the very fabric of reality itself.

In moments of silence, they would engage in collective meditations, allowing their hearts to open even further. With each breath, they anchored more deeply into an intention of love and transformation, sending ripples of this energy outward into the world. Sony guided these meditative journeys, encouraging each member to visualize the new harmonious Earth they wished to co-create. Images of lush landscapes, interconnected communities living in peace, and joyous expressions filled the minds of the participants. They envisioned children laughing, free from the heavy weights of worry or fear, families embracing in unconditional love, and all beings living in harmony with nature. This shared vision sparked a powerful synergy, instilling confidence and clarity of purpose. Sony realized that their community was not merely a gathering of individuals; it was an emerging collective consciousness, each person a vital thread in the grand design of love's tapestry. This connection reassured them that the work they were doing went beyond personal growth; it was a commitment to embodying a new way of being that would affect change far beyond their immediate surroundings.

As the days of gathering unfolded, the community began to manifest the principles they were nurturing within. They created initiatives to support each other, eliciting a profound sense of empowerment. Individuals offered skills, time, and resources to uplift those who might be struggling, transforming their space into a sanctuary of growth and support. Sony watched in awe as neighbors helped each other rebuild, families opened their homes to one another, and laughter became the balm for previous sorrows. Through acts of kindness, they discovered the beauty of connection—the essence of love incarnated in everyday life. Sony was especially moved by how the community actively sought ways to engage with those outside their immediate circle, embracing the principle of extending their hands further into the world. They organized outreach programs, where members could share the love they were cultivating with those who were disconnected from this transformational movement. This ripple effect began to touch lives beyond their gathering space, inspiring others to reflect on their own relationships, beliefs, and the societal structures they participated in.

The journey of collective evolution was not without challenges. Sony recognized that at times, shadows would arise—patterns of fear, segregation, and misunderstanding still lurked within individuals, remnants of a world steeped in division. Sony felt compelled to address these shadows head-on, encouraging dialogues that delved into uncomfortable truths. Rather than shying away from conflict, the community learned that facing it together became an opportunity for growth. They set aside their preconceived notions, engaging in open, compassionate conversations that allowed for healing. Individuals would express their fears, their doubts, and the deeply-rooted conditioning that clung to them, and as they shared these experiences, they would create space for the light of understanding to shine through. It became evident that collective evolution required not only the embrace of love but also the courage to confront what stood in the way of that love. Each conversation acted as a thread of healing, weaving them closer together, fortifying their bonds against the incoming tides of doubt and separation.

At the heart of their transformation lay the realization that each individual was inherently divine, a sacred vessel radiating unique energies that contributed to the greater whole. Sony understood that they were not merely guiding the community; they were part of it, as interconnected as the roots of a great tree entwined beneath the surface. They fostered creative expression through art, music, and dance, inviting each member to channel their essence into these mediums. The vibrant colors on canvases, the melodies that echoed through the air, and the rhythm of their movements encapsulated the love that blossomed among them. The community learned to celebrate their differences, recognizing that diversity was a vital component in their collective evolution. Just as each instrument in an orchestra played its part to create a symphony, so too did each unique individual add depth and richness to their harmonious collective.

As they moved forward, the community began to manifest their visions not just through initiatives but through a profound shift in consciousness. Gathering under the stars on cool evenings, they participated in ceremonies, lighting candles that represented their intentions and the love they held for one another. Each candle flickered with hope, illuminating the path toward a new beginning. In those moments, they understood that the transformation they were witnessing could not be confined to their small circle; it was a beacon of light meant to shine into the world. With each gathering, Sony felt an overwhelming surge of gratitude. They recognized that the love embodied in their community did not merely serve as a shield against the chaos outside; it was a catalyst for deeper understanding and conscious evolution throughout the world.

As time passed, their influence began to ripple through the communities surrounding them. Conversations about love, empathy, and unity became prominent in coffee shops and local parks. People who were once solitary observers began to engage, inspired by the energy radiating from the collective. Sony watched with hope as small groups formed, each becoming a microcosm of the healing work being done. The message of transformation began to expand and find a home within families, workplaces, and schools. Initiatives were taken outside the bounds of their community, establishing connections across neighborhoods, bridging gaps, and fostering relationships built on shared love and compassion. Sony felt their heart swell in joy as they bore witness to the resilience of the human spirit—how, when given the opportunity to love, people could transcend past grievances and work together towards a common purpose. Their community was becoming a living testament to the flourishing potential of the human soul, united in the belief that they could foster a new world, a new Earth.

In the crescendo of their collective journey, Sony felt the weight of their mission heavy upon them, yet pulsing with magnificent potential. They understood that this would be a continuous cycle of growth, both within themselves and their community. Spiritual practice and connection would need to weave through the fabric of their daily lives, nurturing the roots they had planted. As whispers of transformation spread beyond the city limits, there was a clear recognition—the work was not finished. It was merely the beginning of a much grander cycle of awakening and inspiration. The final gathering that led to the collective meditation became a pivotal moment, a culmination of their efforts, a celebration of everything they had manifested together. The community stood side by side, hearts open and spirits entwined, ready to elevate their frequencies through collective love and intention. It was here that Sony truly understood the essence of their commitment: they were a part of the greater whole and, in turn, the greater whole was part of them. Together, they were not just a community; they were a movement, contributing to the evolution of humanity and fostering the dawn of a new harmonious Earth.

A New Beginning

Reflections on the Journey

As the rain pattered softly against the window, each drop resonating with the rhythm of her heartbeat, Sony settled into a moment of deep reflection. The world outside was a tapestry of myriad colors and textures, each shade conveying a nuance of life that Sony had come to appreciate in profound ways. In the presence of this natural beauty, she found herself tracing back the steps that had led her to this pivotal point in her journey, a path strung with lessons that had molded her spirit and reshaped her understanding of existence itself. The transformation within had not been accidental; it was a volitional act of surrender and acceptance to the call of the divine, an echo of the twin flame bond that resonates through all of creation. Each lesson learned felt like a thread woven into the fabric of her being, illuminating the importance of introspection and growth.

Sony thinks back to those early days of uncertainty when the notion of embarking on a spiritual journey felt daunting, almost insurmountable. With every challenge she faced, there came an opportunity for awakening, both personally and collectively. It became clear that as she peeled back the layers of societal conditioning, a deeper wisdom emerged, urging her to acknowledge the light within herself and others. The chaos she observed in the world around her had often clouded her vision, leading her to believe that suffering was an integral part of life. However, the profound truth that began to unfold in her understanding was that suffering arises from separation—from our divine essence, from each other, and from the love that binds us all. This revelation stirred a deep longing to shift perception not just within herself, but to extend that invitation to all those yearning for connection and understanding.

Throughout this passage, Sony encountered various mentors and angels disguised as ordinary people who reflected the wisdom of the universe in their words and actions. Their acceptance and guidance fed the embers of her awakening, reassuring her that she was not alone on this sacred journey. Sony remembers the stillness during moments of deep connection, when the veil of ego lifted, leaving in its wake an indescribable sense of unity. The insights shared by these souls were streams of light, guiding her sails through turbulent waters, helping her learn the essential qualities of unconditional love, empathy, and humility. It was exhilarating and terrifying to realize that love, in its truest form, required vulnerability—the willingness to feel deeply, to create space for others, and to honor differences as paramount for growth.

As Sony earned her stripes through moments of clarity intertwined with darkness, it became evident that within her struggles lay the sacred seeds of healing. Each hardship, every fleeting instance of despair, served as a reminder of her intrinsic power—the ability to choose how she responds to life's myriad challenges. This realization opened up pathways for compassion, allowing her to witness the shared human experience with greater empathy. She found herself more attuned to the narratives spinning around me, unearthing the common threads woven into our stories. This sense of interconnectedness began to illuminate the potential for collective transformation. She began to understand that the shift towards a new harmonious Earth was not a solitary endeavor; it required the concerted effort of all beings willing to cultivate love within themselves and in their communities.

Reflecting on the journey, Sony was reminded of the profound impact of intention. Each thought, each word, and each action rippled through the collective consciousness, borne from the depths of our shared humanity. This was something she felt deeply as she met kindred spirits in unexpected places, attuned to the same call of awakening. Together, we began to create sacred spaces filled with laughter, support, and authenticity. We laughed at our follies, cried openly about our grief, and found strength in our unity, knitting a vibrant tapestry of souls devoted to elevating the frequency of love in our surroundings. The memories of these gatherings became anchors, grounding her in the knowledge that something bigger was at play—a divine unfolding that wasn't merely about personal enlightenment, but a collective renaissance of love and understanding.

Amidst these reflections, the lessons morphed into commitments—by grasping the essence of kindness and generosity, she knew she could start catalyzing change. Understanding that the matrix of separation and control could only be dismantled through love pushed her to channel her energy towards actions rooted in purpose. Concrete steps to nurture a harmonious coexistence became paramount; initiating community discussions, hosting meditation circles, and facilitating acts of kindness were just a few ways of manifesting this intention. Yet she also recognized the rhythm of taking two steps forward, only to experience backsliding. It was crucial to embrace the ongoing nature of this journey as a delicate dance, pivoting between striving and surrendering, success and failure, light and darkness.

As she navigated this continuum of growth, the promise of co-creation enveloped her in its warmth. Sony envisioned a gathering not just of kindred spirits but a convergence of all those who wish to be part of this grand tapestry of love and light, advocating for the reimagining of our world. "Imagine," she pondered in quieter moments, "a world where compassion reigns, where kindness is the preferred currency, and unison triumphs over division." This vision fueled the resolve within her to embrace a leadership role, one cast not in a solitary spotlight, but as a facilitator of connections that spark joy, creativity, and courage. Each person who yearned to join in this collective endeavor was a vital strand, weaving a robust fabric of unity and compassion, bound together by our unique experiences and the desire to contribute to something more significant than ourselves.

Throughout the course of these reflections, it became increasingly clear that the process of awakening was an invitation open to all. The call to action was not just limited to her individual journey but extended to a clarion call for humanity—a gentle nudge beckoning others to embrace the sacredness within them and recognize their innate power. She envisioned her journey as a mirror held up to the world, reflecting the beauty that lay in embracing vulnerability and authenticity, a lighthouse guiding others home to their essence. This was not a path marked by perfection, but rather an intricate dance of pure and honest exploration, one that allowed individuals to turn inward and discover the treasure that rested within.

With renewed vigor bolstered by these lessons, she now sat in a place of invitation, inviting others to gather their courage and step forth into the light of collective spontaneity. The memories of joy, laughter, and purpose experienced amidst newfound connections fortified her resolve to spark gatherings where people would feel safe to explore their true selves—their light and their shadows alike. She visualized meditative rites where we could exchange stories bound by tears and laughter, igniting flames of understanding that would illuminate our paths. The intention was clear; as we delve into our shared narratives and embrace the brilliance of diversity, we would cultivate a space for healing that transcends traditional notions of community, empowering each individual to blossom in their unique way.

The journey ahead held promises yet to be discovered—collective goals were set, and dreams were painted in vivid hues, though they were tempered with the understanding that they would require an ongoing commitment to love and authenticity. With this reflection, she embraced the openness of what was yet to come, welcoming each person on their transformative journey while holding the vision of a new harmonious Earth close to her heart. she recognized that we were co-creators in the truest sense, shaping a reality where peace, love, and empathy would outshine divisive energies, cultivating an environment where every voice was honored and valued.

In closing, she realized that she was only at the precipice of this journey, a continuous spiral of growth beckoning her to explore the depths of existence with awe and reverence. Her reflections had illuminated paths uncharted, reflecting that transformation is a perpetual work of art. And as the heavens wept in confluence with the earth below, she invited others to take up the brush of life and paint our shared destiny together—bold strokes of love, humility, and unity crafting a masterpiece that could inspire generations to come. The unfolding of this new reality rested not solely upon her shoulders, but upon each sacred soul willing to rise and reclaim their power, united in the quest for a harmonious Earth that echoes the rhythm of creation itself. Together, we would weave our destinies amidst the threads of love, transforming dreams into vibrant realities, and creating a canvas that sings the songs of our interconnected hearts.

The Road Ahead

The rain had ceased, leaving behind a world drenched in freshness, each drop bearing witness to the beauty of transformation. Sony stood at the window, gazing out at the vibrant colors of nature awakening from the embrace of the storm. It was in this moment, amid the serene landscape that reflected a deeper truth that they grasped the essence of their journey thus far — a sacred pilgrimage infused with the energy of love and the promise of a new beginning. The past had been a tapestry woven with the threads of self-discovery, challenge, and awakening, and as they reflected on the metamorphosis experienced, it became abundantly clear that this was merely the groundwork laid for an even greater endeavor that lay ahead.

Sony began to map out the steps needed to foster this community of awakened souls. It was clear that nurturing connections required vulnerability, active listening, and a generous spirit. Every encounter presented an opportunity to deepen understanding and engender a culture of support, where individuals felt safe to share their truth, their fears, and their triumphs. The act of sharing one's journey became a sacred ritual; each revelation contributed to the deeper narrative of collective healing, transforming hearts and minds, one story at a time. Along this road ahead, they envisioned workshops and gatherings to celebrate these connections, melding artistic expression with spiritual teachings, enabling a safe space to explore one's energy in the context of community.

Amid this expansion of love and light, Sony recognized that self-care was just as critical. Before they could shepherd others into this new harmonious Earth, they needed to embrace and nurture their own growth. They began to develop a daily practice, a sacred ritual that included meditation and journaling, infusing their existence with clarity and intention. Each morning became an offering—a time to align their heart with the higher frequencies of love and possibility. They knew that the more they cultivated this inner sanctum of peace, the more they would project an aura of hope, inspiring those around them to do the same.

They also felt the pulse of divine guidance coursing through their veins; the whispers of the Divine Presence had echoed in their heart throughout their journey. Each time they stood upon the cusp of fear and uncertainty, the sense of divine support surged forth, emboldening them to persist, trusting that their purpose was both sacred and significant. The concept of surrendering to the flow of universal energy became fiercely alive within them, propelling their journey toward co-creation. It was essential to remain open, allowing inspiration to pour forth and align the threads of their destiny with the greater tapestry of existence.

As Sony envisioned the gathering of like-minded souls, they crafted a beautiful meditative experience that would serve as a catalyst for collective consciousness, a harmonizing frequency that would ripple outwards. This culminating event would coincide with a cosmic alignment, where celestial energies would support the intentions of those who came together with hearts aligned toward love. They prepared to lead this gathering with an open heart, envisioning a circle returned to itself—a configuration that encouraged each participant to not just share, but also receive through the radiant flow of energy that highlighted the interconnectedness of all life.

Ultimately, this was a call to action for every individual reached by their message: to recognize their divine essence, to claim their role in this unfolding journey of transformation, and to take bold steps in nurturing their own light. Sony knew that the energy of love and the echo of unity had the power to heal both individuals and collective spirits. As they prepared to invite others to join in this new chapter, they acknowledged that each person's journey was woven with unique threads, yet each contributed to the collective tapestry. This was the harmony that would elevate humanity, arise from the ashes of division, and create a resilient bond that transcended the constraints of fear.

Through this awakening, Sony would continue to share their knowledge and experiences, fostering a vibrant network of souls committed to transforming the collective narrative towards love, empathy, and understanding. With every step taken along the path, they served as a reminder that they were not alone; together, they were part of a greater movement of ascension—a flourishing ecosystem of sacred souls dedicated to the vision of a new harmonious Earth where hope, compassion, and unity thrived. The road ahead was paved with love; with every stride towards awakening, they would illuminate the path for others, igniting the sharing of wisdom, connection, and ultimately, the reconstruction of a reality steeped in the vibrance and glory of unconditional love.

Inviting Participation

As Sony stands at the precipice of their journey, a sense of profound gratitude envelops them—gratitude for every twist and turn that has led to this moment where clarity dances with purpose. The path has been arduous, filled with moments of uncertainty that tested the very core of their being. Yet, through the labyrinth of personal trials and collective challenges, an undeniable truth has emerged: the work of awakening, healing, and transformation never truly ends; it merely evolves, expanding in scope and depth with each soul that embraces its call. Sony gazes into the shimmering horizon of possibility, a vision painted in hues of hope and potential, where the chaos of the present world can give way to the serenity and unity they long for. It is here, at this crucial juncture, that they feel an impelling urge to turn their gaze outward, reaching beyond the confines of their own experience, extending a heartfelt invitation to all those who yearn for a better world—an open call to participate in this sacred mission of co-creating a new, harmonious Earth.

With a heart swollen by a kaleidoscope of emotions, they reflect on how this journey has been less about the solitary pursuit of enlightenment and more a weaving together of souls, converging on shared intentions and aspirations. Each mentor met along the way has imparted pieces of wisdom, and the kindred spirits encountered have stitched together a vibrant tapestry of relationships that reflect the intricate interconnectedness of life. They recognize that the awakening of one is intimately tied to the awakening of many; every step taken toward love and empathy reverberates through the collective consciousness, creating ripples that can transform communities. The truth is clear: while each individual's journey is uniquely theirs to traverse, the power to create change is exponentially magnified when hearts unite in a common purpose, aligning their energies with the sacred vibrations of love and understanding. It is a call to arms, not in the physical sense but in terms of spirit—the mobilization of those willing to embody principles that transcend the mundane and reach into the realm of the extraordinary.

This invitation is not merely a message conveyed through spoken or written words; it is a resonant echo that calls to those who have felt the stirrings of their own twin flames, those who have witnessed the veils of illusion drop away to reveal the pure light of connection and shared purpose. Sony imagines gathering in open circles, spaces filled with laughter and openness, where all are welcomed to share their stories, their fears, and their aspirations. These gatherings would serve as sacred spaces where the beauty of diversity is celebrated, reminding everyone that there is no singular path to enlightenment, no one-size-fits-all approach to the divine. The diversity of experiences enriches the collective tapestry, inviting the unique frequencies of each twin flame to harmonize with others, creating a symphony of love and understanding that reverberates throughout the universe. They envision events that combine meditation and reflection, each participant radiating the energy of their truth, each unique vibration contributing to the greater whole, culminating in collective creations of healing and hope.

Sony feels an ardent sense of responsibility, realizing that to truly affect change, it is imperative to extend this call beyond the familiar circles of like-minded souls. Engaging with those who might initially resist, those entrenched in the matrix of fear and separation, becomes essential. They ponder the profound potential for awakening that resides within every individual, whether they are currently aware of it or not. It is this awareness that needs cultivating— a gentle prompting that invites curiosity and consideration rather than judgments. Sony reflects on the importance of approaching such individuals with humility, recognizing that each soul is on their own journey, and that our role may simply be to embody the love and acceptance that they seek to inspire in others. It is a delicate balance, a fine line between encouraging participation and respecting individual boundaries, yet the desire to see humanity rise into collective consciousness stirs an unquenchable fire within.

With the wisdom gleaned from mentors echoing in their hearts, Sony resolves to articulate a vision that is clear and engaging, one that invites others to see their own potential as sacred co-creators of this new reality. Through storytelling, art, music, and all forms of expression, they envision a movement blossoming from the seeds of passion, unveiling the beauty of shared experiences and collective creativity. They see workshops igniting sparks of innovation and joy, where participants can learn practical steps for infusing their everyday lives with love and peace, brainstorming ways to foster community resilience in the face of adversity. The engagement of individuals across various platforms— online forums, local community gatherings, and larger global initiatives—would create a mosaic of voices united in the vision of a harmonious Earth, underscoring the essential truth that every contribution, no matter how small, adds irreplaceable value to the collective mission.

As they imprint this grand vision deeply into their consciousness, Sony feels the strength of intention permeating the fabric of the universe, harmonizing with the divine presence that has guided them throughout their journey. They know that this new world is already pulsating in potential, waiting to be unveiled through the collective courage of those willing to stand together in love, acting as conduits for divine transformation. And so, with an open heart and unwavering conviction, they extend their invitation: join in this sacred mission, embrace your divine essence, and together, let us co-create a new harmonious Earth where peace, love, and unity reign supreme. This is not just a call to action; it is a call to connection, to remember that each one of us is an integral part of the greater whole, a vital thread in the tapestry of existence— woven together by love, woven together by life.

www.ingramcontent.com/pod-product-compliance
Lightning Source LLC
Chambersburg PA
CBHW041139120626
46547CB00020B/3043